Writing Naked

MICHAEL MURRAY

Published by Unsolicited Press
www.unsolicitedpress.com
info@unsolicitedpress.com

The author has worked from memory to write these
essays. To respect the privacy of others, some names have
been altered. Some readers may think that they are in this
book – any similarities are just that, mere coincidences.
Unsolicited Press does not know the identities of the people whose names have been changed and request that
readers share in Michael's experiences rather than worry
about where they fit into the narrative. Unsolicited Press
supports Michael Murray's efforts, yet all experiences and
words are the author's alone.

Unsolicited Press Books are distributed by Ingram.
Printed in the United States of America.
Attention schools and businesses: for discounted copies
on large orders, please contact the publisher directly.
ISBN: 978-1-947021-37-2

For Fritz, my stepfather. Thank you for never giving up on me, and for your undying patience, love, support, and grace throughout our journey. This book wouldn't have happened without you.

And for everyone who has ever suffered from anxiety, depression, addiction, or has felt helpless and alone.

Table of Contents

Introduction

The first time I remember thinking that I wanted to write a book happened sometime during high school. I have always been a story teller, and for whatever reason, writing these stories came to me naturally. Finding subjects to write about has never been a challenge. In fact, the only struggle is keeping up with life around me and trying to capture everything that happens as best I can, because these essays and stories are about one thing: life. They are about my life, the lives of others, and their relationship to me.

I went to school for roughly six years to study writing with the sole intention of publishing my own book one day; a book that would tackle the hard truths—one that would address and wrestle with love, loss, depression, and ultimately tackle my own consciousness.

When I secured the contract to write this book, I was beyond elated. But once I realized that while I had earned the chance to tell my stories, I now actually had to do it! I became very nervous, anxious, and genuinely terrified. Emotional roller-coasters are my favorite kind of ride, so take your Dramamine now. I remember asking the last professor I had at Portland State, "How do I do this? What if people are upset by what I write? What if they hate me after reading it?"

I knew that what I would eventually write would be intense, that it would be disturbing to some. But I hoped that by sharing my own turbulent journey of navigating depression, alcoholism, anxiety, and anger, it might help others feel a little less alone in their own struggles.

Truth be told, I am not a reader. People ask how this is even possible. Well, I struggle with reading, I always have. My mind wanders off the page and I lose my place, sometimes reading for pages and forgetting what I read. I used to be terrified of reading aloud because I was so scared and insecure that I would pronounce something wrong, or that people would notice my lisp more. On the rare occasion that I find myself at a book store, I almost always wind up in the cooking section. I love cooking and can read recipes and make perfect sense of what's happening and what the outcome will be. It's not the same with the writing of this book.

I had all the ingredients for this book scattered around my head—memories, anecdotes, music, food, feelings, etc. I had no idea where to begin. I thought of buying a dry erase board and writing potential stories or prompts on it and picking one a day to write on...that never happened. I would write ideas down in the notes app on my phone but oftentimes I would do this drunk, and when I'd try to recall them, I'd forget what I was intending to do with them in the first place.

It wasn't until about a year ago when I read the book *So Sad Today* by Melissa Broder that I realized how I would attempt to write my book. *So Sad Today* was given to me as a gift and, like most of my books, was initially used as a means of collecting dust. Then it came up on a required reading list for my final course at Portland State. I cracked it open and read almost all of it in one sitting. I was floored by Broder's brutally raw delivery of her struggles with the same things I was trying to make sense of. She wrote so honestly about her personal life without any apologies. It was like climbing into the mind of an incredibly brilliant woman my age who had experienced tragedy, loss, fear, insecurity, and of course, sadness, and was putting it all out there with no holds barred. I couldn't get over how brave her writing was, and it ultimately gave me the strength to sit down and attempt to do the same. I was going to write the way I thought, and I was going to let people see it.

Something that Broder wrestles with on the page is substance abuse. Toward the end of the book she writes about getting sober, invites anyone that needs help to seek it, and provides her personal email. This was huge to me. I have always known that I've needed to stop drinking, and I didn't want my book to suffer from it, so I stopped. I have a glass of wine with dinner when I'm eating something worthy, but other than that, I haven't been drunk in months. Writing this book has helped me not drink. My mind slowly became clearer, my anger has dissipated as well as my anxiety. I have my moments, but I am much, much happier. So, writing this book has brought me some peace.

When I asked my professor those questions about how people might react, he said, "Michael, you'll never be able to please everyone, and you will offend some people, you might even lose some people you thought were your friends along the way. But as long as you write the truth, nothing else matters."

Writing Naked is my heart and soul poured out onto the page. It's all I've ever wanted, and I can't thank those who have helped me along the way enough.

Please enjoy my book. If you're struggling, I hope something inside these pages helps you to feel a little less alone.

Michael Murray

Foreword

Aside from driving around Cleveland in our parents' cars, renting movies from Blockbuster, and staying up late entertaining our Catholic school curiosities, my earliest collaboration with Michael Murray was an idea to co-author a children's book for adults [cue eye-rolls]. I'll save us both the embarrassment of disclosing what this publication might have included because luckily that was not the book Michael was meant to write.

He wasn't ready to claim his aloneness, the feelings of not belonging. He wasn't ready for *Writing Naked* just yet. There were still stories to be collected, some involving being actually naked—dancing naked, passing out naked, cooking naked—a slew of mistakes to be made, and a resolve to be had. He needed to first delve into the high level of emotional awareness that accompanies anxiety and depression, fuck shit up a bunch, and stay with the pain so that he might also experience the joy and peace that comes along to soothe the singed places in our souls.

Even as kids, we got to know anxiety and depression, shame and guilt, and what it sounds like/smells like/tastes like/aches like to feel everything. Today, it is part of my job to encourage people with anxiety to see the ways that having a high level of emotional intelligence actually serves their life and the lives of those around them...but the harsh, in-the-moment truth is that when you have anxiety you feel all the pain and all the joy so strongly that it leaks out of your eyes at inconvenient times and drools off your lips and sounds like *I love you* and *I hate you* and it buzzes in your ears and crawls under your skin and burns into the backs of your eyelids when you press them together so tightly they almost push the eyeballs into the space where your brain-mush is firing away in all directions at all times.

And you might, as Michael did, begin to feel filled up by the dramatic. He has always been a lover of drama, because it was there that he felt most at home; in the presence of suffering. Where there was none, he would create it himself. A symptom of the anxious-minded is writing the ending before it comes; a dramatic and tragic ending no less. I suppose it's also a symptom of being a writer.

There are patterns that give us a sense of safety. It is safe to assume the worst will happen, because when it does, you get to be right. And when we believe that the only ending will be a tragic one, we do everything in our power to prove ourselves right. You get the validation that the universe is harsh, and all the good people die and the bad ones too and all the girls fuck hotter dudes and it shouldn't matter because you fucked other girls too but it does because your heart is always breaking and you are always seeking more and more validation for why you feel lost, empty, alone, and sad.

It's our job to throw a wrench in that cycle. Somehow, we fool ourselves into thinking that not only dreams, but normalcy, sanity, will be served to us on silver platters with a glass of Pinot Noir to wash it down. If we can relearn any lesson from Michael Murray it's that if you are waiting for someone else to save you, you're probably in the wrong place. The patterns in our lives are often ones of our own making. Only when we begin to allow life to happen for us, do we find it in our capacity to shift. But of course, that part of the story happens later.

While most of the world spends time skinny dipping in the cesspool of indifference toward the human condition, after thirty-one years of being with himself, Michael Murray decided to invite us to a brazen, grand-tour of his very own brain-space broken record...the repetitive pain, failure, heartbreak, self-medicating and numbness, rapid-firing between each neuron, rubbed raw.

It may have begun as an act of self-service, or as he might say "the longest suicide note ever written," but what shows up between the lines in *Writing Naked* is an invitation to move in closer. By putting his own humanity on display, in all its supposed flaws, the result is less about punishment or redemption and more about a deeper understanding of how we all need to be loved.

Traveling in Indonesia during the writing of this book, Michael coerced me into swimming in the ocean after dark one night. All I could envision were giant grey fins and the foreboding "dun dun dun dun dun dun" *Jaws* theme music. Not to mention the death-trap coral reef I was bare-footedly unprepared for...and in my underwear no less—but I went in.

Within seconds of floating in the black water, I felt the first sting. And then another. Jellyfish all around. I flailed helplessly, cutting my foot on the coral below, my left side on fire, and as I looked around I saw not an outstretched hand or a guiding headlamp to usher me out of this oceanic hell, but the moon-lit, bare-assed backside of Michael, scrambling onto the shore already some twenty yards away. I heard him yell something (likely some snarky comment about beached whales) as I made my way to the sand and assessed the damage.

When he finally sauntered over, with a towel, a beer, and a forced smile—testament to his hope that I'd let this one slide—I hissed, "Where the F did you go?!"

My side had already stopped burning, my panic was subsiding, a reminder of the only guarantee in this life: impermanence. But I kept to my anger and frustration over his abandoning me there to die. It is a funny thing, impermanence. It should be the very reason we let go, knowing that there is something newly available to us in each moment of our lives.

But instead, it is usually why we are driven to desperately hold on.

He squeezed me timidly. "I was scared. And I knew you were good. If you needed help, you would have asked."

I saw his vulnerability then; his willingness to show up in honesty. And I realized that my truth was that I was okay on my own. *Writing Naked* assumes the same of everyone who reads it: you are okay, enough and capable on your very own. These essays remind us that we are all scared. Scared to be seen, to show up as ourselves, to ask for help when we really need it. We're scared of getting stung. But maybe we can take solace in the fact that we are not alone in our fear.

Michael's writing is a tribute and a calling to those of us who are crippled by our own fear of showing up as exactly who we are. Through the common and uncommon experiences that undeniably change us, we are all connected here. If this is your first time too, doing this human experience thing, *Writing Naked* will show you that it's okay to still be figuring it out. We are each so very insignificant in the grand scheme of existence, except in our hearts where, of course, we are infinite. It is from that place where we can choose to cultivate courage, as Michael has.

Have you ever heard the expression "if it doesn't open, it's not your door"? Here's an updated version inspired by *Writing Naked*: If you want to get through, slamming your head against the door repeatedly like a drunk idiot only leaves you bruised with a fat head. The key needed to open the door to the rest of your life might look like courage or forgiveness or even acceptance. It may take you thirty-one years or three weeks or your entire lifetime to find that key, but this book will dare you to stay long enough to find your own way through.

The only way through this life after all, is to stay, for a time. To be brave enough to know yourself, and, in this rare case of *Writing Naked*, to share what paths you tripped down, throwing that rascal, ego, in front of the bus of authenticity. This is a book of stories sweating with human insecurity, crippling anxiety, open-hearted love and fear, blinding anger, steadfast connection, substance/self-abuse and the guilt of being a bystander to human pain. What we might find is that it isn't so much about what happened, or didn't happen, what was broken or fixed or neglected, but the meaning we distill; the visceral reaction we share when staring the human condition in the face.

Ultimately, *Writing Naked* is about bravery. About standing up, taking off all your clothes and jumping into the darkest ocean. It's about yelling (or whispering), "this is who I am, these are my mistakes." It's about finding out where judgment really comes from. About the eternal struggle each of us faces when we come to a fork where both roads lead us down a way not totally our own, where the ground is crumbling and narrow and unforgiving, and we

16

know that we don't belong. But somehow, these are the paths that lead us home.

Get naked.

Hanna Kokovai
Novice Human

Writing Naked

MICHAEL MURRAY

Happy Hour with the Universe

Me: Hey, you're all-knowing, right? Can I ask you something?

Universe: As long as it's not "what's the meaning of life..." It's been a long day.

Me: I've seen *Hitchhiker's Guide to the Galaxy*. I'm satisfied with "42." My question is closer to home—I want to know why I drink, and why I can't stop.

Universe: Do you really think you can't stop?

Me: That's how it feels. I don't even get what drinking does for me, aside from exacerbating my anger, laying the foundation for bad decisions, sending me into an anxious sinkhole and sucking the life out of the 24-48 hours following... do I really think it's that fun?

Universe: Ok. Let's start with this: Can you remember when you started drinking?

Me: Yeah, I was about fifteen.

Universe: I remember a lot of your friends had already started before then, while you were just smoking pot.

Me: I was freaked out by the image of being drunk at first. It looked scary to me, watching my friends falling all over the place, but I guess it was just a matter of time before I was falling all over the place too. Once I started, I drank like most kids; we'd rifle through random parent's liquor supplies and take a little from each bottle and end up with gross concoctions that we'd plow through just to get to the drunk part. We'd ride our bikes to Russo's grocery store and buy various food flavorings used for baking; they contain mostly alcohol so if we bought six orange extracts and mixed them with orange soda, we'd have a pretty decent (disgusting) orange cocktail. One thing was universal for all of us: we were drinking to get as fucked up as possible.

Universe: The reason was different for each of you though.

Me: You're right, and for me it was easier to play the part of shitfaced goofball than the part of child of a broken home. The same time I started to drink hard and use drugs harder was the same time that my parents split up. And I was the only one.

Universe: When your dad took you to Coventry and bought you those Phish CDs and then told you he was leaving your mom, that was devastating.

Me: Yeah. I can remember being very angry and embarrassed. I didn't tell anyone what was going on. I started smoking a lot more pot, as much as I could get a hold of. Eventually the word got out that Mike and Karin Murray were splitting up, and other parents forbid their kids from hanging out with me. So, I started hanging out with older kids and it was easier for them to get booze, so it was easier for me. Plus, I was smoking so much pot and missing so much class that eventually I was drug tested and I was kicked out of my first high school.

Universe: And instead of backing off, that's when the drinking really started to go next level.

Me: I was angry, hurt, scared, and embarrassed. Not to mention, because of my expulsion from the first high school, my parents started drug testing me regularly, so I started drinking more. I drank because I didn't want to feel...or think. I was exhausted by the constant feeling and thinking. Fourteen years later I guess I do it for the exact same reason.

Universe: Sounds like we've established a pattern and a source. Tell me more about what you didn't want to feel or think about.

Me: Jesus. I need a drink.

Universe: ...which brings us back to the question of whether you CAN'T stop, or simply choose not to.

Me: Shit, I didn't want to think about the fact that my parents were splitting up. I would watch them walk across the bridge to "talk" from an upstairs bathroom in our house and I could hear them screaming at one another. It killed me. Seeing my dad pack his things and move out was an entirely new level of emotion. I didn't want to think about how I was failing in school and how I was getting kicked out, being forced to attend public school with a bunch of strangers; mostly entitled, rich, Jewish kids whose parents didn't give a shit what they did. I didn't want to think about how my true friends' parents were forbidding them to hang out with me because I was a part of an imperfect home. I didn't want to feel the truth of what I had become, in other people's eyes: an outcast; a scapegoat; the reason why their sons and daughters were drinking or smoking; the kid with the messed-up life.

Universe: I know there was at least one good thing you gained despite losing a lot during that time.

Me: Yeah, that's when I met Jon.

Universe: You two hit it off right away.

Me: We met at this party and talked the whole night about our parents, how we felt. I knew it was safe to tell him, somehow. We smoked a bunch of weed and crushed beers and when the party ended, he came back to my mom's house to spend the night. We pretty much lived together from then on.

Universe: Right off the bat you two were partying pretty hard together. You found someone on the same plane as you to get fucked up with?

Me: Yeah, but to me it was much more. I had found someone who I could relate to. We were the only people each other knew whose parents were splitting up. He was someone I could confide in, even if we were just self-medicating.

Universe: Did you know it was "self-medicating" at the time?

Me: I don't know, I was fourteen or fifteen. I likely didn't even know what that meant. Whatever it was, it didn't save Jon in the end. And I was alone again.

Universe: Yes, you were.

Me: To a certain extent, one of the main reasons I drink is because I started when I was fifteen and it's been the only way I know to navigate this world, by numbing myself to it. It's easier to drink, or at least that's what I've fooled myself into believing. I drink because I tell myself it's all that I know. It was the first tool I found, and the one I've continued to use all this time. I started half my lifetime ago, and I only "quit" once.

Universe: Involuntarily.

Me: Yeah, not by choice! I wasn't anywhere near mature enough to have made a choice like that on my own. When I was sent away to boarding school right after Jon died, I simply couldn't drink there. It wasn't impossible, but I was living so isolated from the rest of the world that it just wouldn't have been worth it to try.

Universe: You thought about it though.

Me: Oh sure I did, but it would have been a major pain in the ass. I'd have to leave campus, wander down the street and hopefully find some local Maine fuck-ups to buy me beer from the gas station. A lot of other students tried this, some were successful, others got robbed and beat up. Some kids would drink mouthwash in their dorm rooms and steal cooking sherry from the kitchen. This seemed disgusting to me and they always got caught. It wasn't worth it. For some reason, all that was beneath me.

Universe: Even when your friend sent you those cigarettes, it was a disaster.

Me: Hah, yeah, when I would wander down to the ocean and chain-smoke three cigarettes and try to cover up the smell with Axe body spray, that was ridiculous- beyond that I didn't do shit, well, besides my twenty-minute Ambien trips on my top bunk of my dorm.

Universe: Can you remember how it felt being sober?

Me: Well, it ebbed and flowed, I'd go home for breaks and the first thing I would do is get as fucked up as possible. Once, I remember it was my first time returning to Cleveland, and I was flying out of Boston. I had a friend who was a freshman at Boston College. I was staying with her until I left for my flight and she had bought me a bottle of Jim Beam and some smokes, so I had those waiting for me. When I got to her dorm I drank Jim Beam and Red Bulls, one of Jon and my favorite drinks. I barely remember that, but it did happen. I suppose that in the year and a half that I was at boarding school, I was only sober when I was at school, so stretches of three to four months.

Universe: And in those month-stretches of sobriety, how did you feel?

Me: I didn't.

Universe: Explain, if you weren't self-medicating, you should have been feeling plenty...

Me: In the months that I wasn't using, I was being fed a concoction of pills a local shrink in Maine had prescribed me.

Universe: Ah, that's right!

Me: Every morning, afternoon, and evening, myself and most of the other students would shuffle down a path to the "medical building" where we'd line up, just like in *One Flew Over the Cuckoo's Nest*, and we'd be handed a little paper cup with our various drugs. My daily regiment was:

<u>Morning</u>: Paxil, Adderall, and Klonopin
<u>Noon</u>: Adderall, Klonopin
<u>Evening</u>: Ambien

The nurse failed miserably at making sure we swallowed everything, so we could share meds, and of course everyone did. Once I learned that if I chewed up the Ambien and let it dissolve and fought the sleep I so desperately needed, I could get a kind of drunk and buzzy feeling, but it only lasted so long.

Universe: Interesting.

Me: How is it interesting? You're the Universe. Shouldn't you know all of this?

Universe: Yes, Michael Murray, I am the UNIVERSE. Everything that you have told me thus far, I already know, but I know you, and I know you're dramatic and you need to explain everything to the point of minutia, so consider the last few minutes of conversation to be your "play time." You got it out of your system, now let me ask you some questions more to the point.

Me: You're right, god dammit, shoot.

Universe: Do you want to stop drinking?

Me: Yeah.

Universe: What makes this time different? Because I know you've said that before.

Me: I think and say it almost every time I get regrettably drunk. And every time I get drunk is regrettable. So, yeah, I want to stop all the time. It's a cycle of shame and regret, moments of perceived fun, and the impending doom that comes with a realization that I can't control myself.

Universe: How deep is your self-awareness around what happens when you drink?

Me: About as deep as the carafe of sangria I want to crush right now from talking about this.

Universe: Cute. So, tell me what goes on in your head as you drink?

Me: Well, I guess I'd break it down into three phases. The first sip of the first drink sends waves of relief and bliss across my lips. It's exciting. It's like quenching a feeling more than a thirst, like I'm returning to something that I had missed or forgotten. The first three drinks, let's say they're sangrias, or jalapeño margaritas, or gin and grapefruit juices with rhubarb bitters, give me a bubbly and excitable feeling. I felt bubbly and excited just saying that. I'm social and eager to talk and tell jokes or make humorous jabs at myself…it's the fun part.

Universe: Humorous jabs, eh?

Me: Yeah, it's my self-deprecating sense of humor that tries to mask the contempt I have for myself, usually because I'm drinking. It's funny for probably five minutes.

Universe: Yeah, I know. It's kind of hard to watch, because I know what comes next…

Me: Yep, the next three drinks, which could be a bottle of rosé, or more gin and juice variations usually start getting my brain churning. I start noticing my anxiousness. It's like a closet door that I've managed to keep closed and hide all the tangled-up extension cords inside, somehow comes unhinged and all the piled-up shit in there starts tumbling out at my feet. I start to become hyper aware of what I'm saying and how it sounds and I become insecure and cagey and I realize that I'm starting to talk out of my ass.

Universe: What happens next?

Me: Thinking, over-thinking, getting caught up in the cords. At some point, I'll hone in on the fact that I should probably quit in this moment, but instead I move onto the next phase of drinking.

Universe: Which is?

Me: Being a dick. I start to project my insecurity outward and it manifests itself as anger and contempt. I'll overhear someone say something that I think is stupid and I'll judge them and criticize them in my mind. Sometimes I'll even call someone out just to make myself feel better about the fact that I am hating myself for the way that I am behaving. All the while I know that I am becoming more drunk and less in control and the only answer I have is to move on and drink more to try and counteract the feelings of insecurity.

Universe: Ok, you start to drink more because you're drinking and you don't like what's happening?

Me: Haha, yes, exactly. Literally chasing myself down a hole of self-punishment and frustration from drinking because I drink. I start to get angry with myself so I move onto the final phase: blackout. I can't tell you how I function during this phase, but somehow I retain enough motor control to cause some type of scene, send angry text messages, sleep with random and unavailable women, etc. Just a few weeks ago I passed out at the bar of the restaurant I manage and woke up in a booth I'd been carried to by a co-manager just as breakfast service was starting. I find out about what I've done the next day, which I suppose is ACTUALLY the final phase: shame.

Universe: Seems exhausting.

Me: I'm tired. I feel like I am constantly waking up from a restless night, with glimpses of things I've created out of anger, shame, guilt and frustration, all set into motion by that first sip. I've been waiting for something catastrophic to happen to have what I would deem a good enough reason to stop.

Universe: Do you think it might be a good idea to decide what would constitute a total catastrophe? Like, your version of the apocalypse.

Me: The truth is that there have already been so many catastrophic reasons to stop, but I haven't. When I'm triggered—by stress, boredom, loneliness—I'm not thinking about potential outcomes, or the last bad thing I conjured out of drunkenness.

Universe: How do these triggers manifest themselves in your day-to-day life?

Me: Jesus! I feel like I'm answering one of those stupid iPad questionnaires they hand me every time I check into the psych unit at the Cleveland Clinic. I hate those goddamn things.

Universe: Yeah, I know, I was there when you threw a temper tantrum at the reception desk because you claimed that if someone *wasn't* depressed, filling out the questionnaire would surely do the trick.

Me: I thought that was hilarious!

Universe: You're a child.

Me: Obviously.

Universe: So... tell me about stress, boredom, loneliness.

Me: Well, first of all, I have a serious problem with what my sister calls FOMO, or "fear of missing out..."
Universe: No shit.

Me: Plus, I don't like being alone, and my go-to is usually heading to a bar. I never really learned how to enjoy "being in the present" as they say. I get caught up in what happened or what could happen, never what's happening right now. So, it's brunches filled with gin and grapefruit juice, afternoon mingling with rose when it's hot out and evenings of mezcal margaritas, manhattans, and wine to counter the aloneness. Being alone for me means being bored and being bored and alone means that all I have are my own thoughts, which you know, are not my favorite.

Universe: Drinking is about distraction and socializing then?

Me: Yeah, except even when I go to bars, in reality I'm going alone. I trick myself into thinking it's normal to make $300 and then go buy a bottle of single malt and drink the entire thing, as if there is some sort of sophistication in it. Sitting at a bar by myself doesn't feel lonely because I know every bartender in my neighborhood. I'm going to "visit my friends." Mostly I keep the company of people that humor me and listen to my drunken ramblings and perhaps find me amusing and a little mysterious.

Universe: Do you think you're amusing and mysterious?

Me: Only if those are euphemisms for idiotic and predictable. People sometimes think I'm entertaining until the darkness sets in and I self-deprecate and spout depressing shit that people don't know what to do with so they brush it off. A lot of my humor is mixed with self-hate and shame, and since I know you're going to ask why I have self-hatred and shame, well, it's mostly because I'm an alcoholic.

Universe: This is the first time that you've referred to yourself as an alcoholic.

Me: So?

Universe: It's just interesting.

Me: Why? I am an alcoholic. I've never denied that.

Universe: How do you define an alcoholic?

Me: I once heard someone say an alcoholic is a person who drinks as much as I do that I don't like.

Universe: Hilarious, but how do you define yourself as one?

Me: I am someone that cannot simply drink in moderation. If I even have a sip of booze, I'm in for the long haul. I've never had "one drink."

Universe: Have you given any thought to what might be true if you were sober?

Me: Since I started drinking I can honestly say that I've only been operating at 50% of my true potential and capacity. I've been numbing myself to life because I don't know how to deal with it. For instance, I never really dealt with Jon dying or my parents' divorce. I've never dealt with my emotions, I've buried them with booze. Clarity scares me. I might be scared by what I find in my sober brain.

Universe: What else scares you?

Me: Everything. I'm scared of losing people or places, letting go of the things that feel safe. I'm scared I won't get laid because sober sex lacks the social lubricant I use to project false confidence, seem fun and pick up women. I'm scared of falling in love and having to live up to something more than being a drunk disappointment. I'm scared of never finding out the difference between alone and lonely. I am scared of finding out who my friends truly are, who I really am...I'm scared of what it would look like to try happiness.

Fear and Loathing on Social Media

"Here's a picture of me wearing fancy Icebreaker Merino Wool clothing at the top of a summit I climbed."

Not pictured: The 12 drinks I drowned myself in the night before. The Adderall I took to counter my hangover and get my ass moving. Also, the 10 extra pounds hiding under that puffy coat, a physical testament to the fact that I certainly do not climb mountains on the daily.

"Here's a picture of a beautiful meal I prepared with Dungeness Crab I bought from the Japanese food market."

Not pictured: The $90 I had to spend to create this #foodpic and the subsequent overdraft fee that arrived from my bank a few days later.

"Here's a picture of me at the coast surfing. Look how rad I am! #ilivewhereyouvacation!"

Not pictured: What I did with the remaining 23 hours of my day which included snorting some coke in the parking lot of the Screw & Brew, spending 70 imaginary dollars on Margaritas and Bourbon, blacking out and passing out in my trunk.

"Here's a picture of me on a friend's boat where I look really skinny! Look how much fun I'm having!"

Not pictured: My strict diet regimen of booze and cocaine, which was likely a contributing factor in my not actually remembering this day at all.

"Here's a cute picture of my mom and I on a whale watching tour in the San Juan Islands!"

Not pictured: My suicidal thought process that caused me to beg my mom to plan on visiting for a month to save me from myself.

"Here's a picture of my girlfriend and I on East 4th dressed up for a fancy event! Look how hot my girlfriend is and look how perfect we are together!"

Not pictured: The (admittedly beautiful) benefit for the Arthritis Foundation we were attending, which I proceeded to ruin with my raucous blackout behavior, including mouthing off and trying to fight some rich douche bag. Oh, and the handcuffs the cops needed to escort me out of the event while my girlfriend cried on the curb.

"Here's a picture of me on the 4th of July, dressed in red white and blue holding a half-stick of dynamite my friend got me. Don't I look fun?"

Not pictured: The unsuspecting lady walking down the street with her dog, who was nearly killed by the tree that fell after I got piss-wasted and blasted it with the dynamite.

"Here's a picture of me on a cool hike, having my picture taken by my adventure buddies!"

Not pictured: The stranger I enlisted to take this staged photo. The various breweries I was drinking at alone all day. Me, nursing my anxieties and getting just drunk enough to entertain the debate between driving my car into Hood River and deciding that now wasn't a good time to off myself because when the tox-screen came back on my corpse they'd dub my death an "accident". And I couldn't have people finding out that I was just a drunk.

On social media, *I'm the fucking king of the world*—I totally have my shit together. I live in Portland. I hang with super rad people. I'm a lead bartender at a place that everyone loves. You can see me 'checking in' to all the coolest events in town, eating oysters, having adventures, being tall and tan and tough.

I work hard, too. I've worked hard at every job I've ever had. I've never taken a sick day, not even from this job of image maintenance. So it makes sense that I'd work hard at covering up the IRL version of me; the version that snorts coke at work every night and drives home high, usually stopping at Popeye's and smashing an entire box of fried chicken; the version that considers shooting pool a sufficient form of exercise; the version that lays on the couch sucking down nitrous, methodically checking/posting to all the social media platforms and jerking off until I fall into what I'd consider sleep, but thanks to the Vyvanse I'm taking to keep my ADHD in check, is really just resting my eyes for a bit while my brain does the un-happy dance until the sun comes up. Then I do it all over again. It's exhausting. But it's worth it. If someone I have become obsessed with or attached to the idea of sleeping with were to find out who I am behind the image, I'd implode. I'm safe right here, as a social chameleon.

I can morph into whatever you want me to be: a yoga instructor, a Phish fan, a skier, a poet, a musician, a world traveler, a volunteer, a drunk...and I'm good at it. I am charming to the point of manipulation. If there's one thing I know, it's people. I've been told that I'm a collector of people. I need them. I wonder how many of my collection would stick around if I decided to tell them exactly what was going on inside this crazy, depressed head of mine. *What if I told them how I really felt? What if I showed them?*

In my Facebook bio, I list only the colleges I'm proud of. I lie about the dates of graduation because I don't want people to know I was held back a year in high school, and then took my sweet time obtaining a college degree that I can use to prove my success. I only list the jobs that seem cool, like working at a rad bar, or volunteering in South America.

I've deleted Facebook and Instagram several times. My plan is always the same: deactivate, never return. I imagine spending my newfound time abundance doing things like actually going outside for more than a back-alley piss, being active, taking a long-term approach to addressing my Dad Bod, being happier. It never sticks.

Recently, I booked a trip to Bali with a friend I've known my whole life that I'm ACTUALLY in love with, not just obsessed with. In anticipation of the venture, I went down a YouTube rabbit hole looking at travel vlogs, many of them "amateur" Go-Pro videos made by couples. The first one starts with a POV shot of a beautiful woman laying (assumingly) naked in a bed that overlooks the ocean. We're then catapulted into a series of clips from what I am led to believe is their "freedom lifestyle," not just a short-term vacation. The couple is insanely good looking. The woman has what most people consider to be a perfect body. She's wearing thong bathing suit bottoms in every shot with a perfect ass and her tits are about to fall out of what little is holding them. Her male counterpart is a chiseled bleach-blond surfer. Pretty much every shot is showcasing their bodies, along with other model-like playmates they meet at various waterfalls, clubs, beaches, etc.

I kept thinking, "Fuck man, you're gonna look like a slob compared to these people, you're gonna be that fat American that's hanging out with a beautiful girl who any one of these surf bros would love to bang." *Jesus*. I couldn't come off it. I thought about how much time I have until I leave for my trip (24 days). I thought about how I might start taking more Adderall to suppress my appetite. I thought, "Ok, just don't drink booze or eat meat or cheese or bread for 24 days and at least you'll shed some weight. God knows you're not gonna go to a gym." I thought, "I really hope she doesn't bring a Go-Pro. I'm not ready for video."

All the time I've spent stalking, creeping, judging, hating and missing has just confirmed what I've known to be true since the first time I was asked to choose a profile pic: it's all a lie, and we all play along. Imagine what a traitor to humanity I'd be if instead of commenting with a peppy "miss you so much!" or a thumbs-up or laugh-til-I-cry emoji, I left this in the comments section: *Hey, this picture is super fancy, but why didn't you post the one of yourself from that night when I saw you blacked out when you knocked over an entire rack of Riedel wine glass-es and then attempted to make out with your friend's dad? That was pretty fucked. I'd love to see more of what you're actually like. Cool, enjoy your hangover. I'm proud of you!*

I see attempts at transparency, like, before and af-ter pictures of people who've done a cleanse or the Whole 30 challenge. They want people to see that they're being brave by showing their progress. Good for them. But where are the photos of the people who are still in the "before" phase, with no intention of morphing into a filter-heavy "after" any time soon?

I see pictures of friends and their kids at weddings wearing pastel pinks and blues and I wonder how they even have the energy, when I know their mar-riage is a disaster, their kids are already out of control and two years from now I'll be sitting at a bar with one of them commiserating about single life. I hope they prove me wrong by staying together, buying that house, taking those vacations and posting all about it, so that I can just continue the cycle of com-parison, impersonation and self-defeat, while they actually live out their social media lives. But some-how, I doubt it.

Social media is more or less the basis on which I compare myself to myself and to others; it's pictures of me doing things that I know other people will "Like." I'm a master of disguise, just like everyone else. I'm not better than these people though. On social media, no one is better than anyone—it's a level playing field where everyone is full of fear and loathing into the wee hours of the night all around the world.

You can follow me on Instagram @writingnaked.

Cast Away in Maine

The first time I visited Maine was to check out a boarding school that came recommended by a behavioral health physician at the Cleveland Clinic. So, there's that. My parents and I took a little field trip there to participate in what was described to me as an interview. I stayed in a hotel room with my dad at a place across the highway from the Holiday Inn, where my mom stayed. I wasn't speaking with my mom for various reasons. I don't think we talked the entire way there. I don't think we talked until the interview.

The interview, as it was, consisted of my parents and I sitting in a stately room in a building called "The Mansion" with two men, one, the headmaster of the school, the other, a teacher who had just taken the role as the head of the wilderness school. I didn't know it yet, but I was going to be one of three guinea pigs for the wilderness program that the school was launching.

At this point, this entire scenario was a joke to me. My parents had threatened to send me away for a while, and the shrinks at the Cleveland Clinic, in my mind, were doing the same. It didn't occur to me that they'd actually go through with it.

So, I'm sitting in this room with these two men, with my guard fully up. They began with the question, "Michael, in your opinion, why are you sitting in this room?" What my answer was, I can't say, but some fourteen years later, I can say what it should have been:

My parents are getting divorced and they hate each other.

My best friend just killed himself in the most disturbing way possible.

I got tossed out of school for smoking pot.

I've been smoking too much pot, skipping school, drinking, taking pills, cheating on my girlfriend, blacking out, getting arrested, and hating everyone around me, mostly myself.

I'm an angry, extremely emotional kid with a lot of pain and trauma and I'm sitting in this room because my parents are worried I'm either going to kill myself or overdose.

Thirty-year-old me earned the above perspective on seventeen-year-old me. I hate seventeen-year-old me. I feel bad for seventeen-year-old me. I feel bad for thirty-year old me.

The interview wasn't an interview at all. There was no "acceptance or denial." I was in denial.

Everyone was worried about me. These two strange men yelled at me for the better part of two hours and told me that I needed to shape up. I was just a kid—a very angry and sad kid. The rest of the interview consisted of a lot of crying.

I was such a mess then that it's hard to remember what happened after. I disappeared when I got back to Cleveland. I was barely going to school. An entire community of people were blaming me and hating me for my best friend's suicide. I blamed myself for him killing himself. I blamed myself because everyone else was blaming me. I blamed myself because I felt that I really was responsible.

What I do remember is "accidentally" signing into my dad's email one day as I was still logged in on an old-school Mac; what child of my generation has not set up their parent's email account? The very first email was from one of the men from the interview. I opened it and it read something like, "Don't let Michael know that he is going to come here, he will more than likely run away and cause a huge scene."

They were right.

I fired off a paragraphs-long email from my dad's account letting them know that there was no way I was going to come there. I tried to sound intelligent. One line went something like, "Your petty attempts to ensnare me into your fucked up little school fall off of me like raindrops...you'll never see me again."

I'd be back in Maine a month later.

For the weeks leading up to my departure date, I made myself scarce. Feeling the need to push back against the unfairness of being sent away, I stayed with various people whom my parents didn't know. I felt betrayed and very tired.

I hadn't lived at my mom's house for months, but on the morning of my surrender I told all my friends to meet me there to say goodbye. When I arrived, I saw that all my things had already been packed. There was also a pile of camping equipment next to the piano I'd never seen before: new boots, a head-lamp, a raincoat, wool socks, and some rain pants. I couldn't imagine why I'd need any of this; I was going to a boarding school, not camping. At that point in my life I couldn't have pointed to the state of Maine on a map.

One of the last things I remember is kissing my girlfriend goodbye and playing my piano for a bit. My dad drove me to the airport. I got suitably high before getting in the car and pulling out of my mom's driveway to the sight of all of my friends standing in the driveway waving at me. None of them were smiling; everyone was sad but everyone was also relieved.

My dad and I flew to Manchester, New Hampshire, and then drove to Maine in a rental car. We got a room at the same hotel where we stayed for the interview, went to Shaw's grocery store, bought a bottle of Jim Beam and two packs of Marlboro Lights, went back to the hotel and drank bourbon and smoked cigarettes.

He dropped me off at the boarding school steps the next morning, we cried, hugged, and parted ways. Inside the mansion there was a large room in the front of the building with couches and whatnot. It was an old Victorian with lots of furniture and lamps that looked like they belonged in either a funeral home or your great grandma's estate sale.

The two men from the interview were there to greet me along with two kids in uniforms similar to what I wore to Catholic School. I remember exactly what I was wearing: New Balance sweatpants, long sleeve tie-dye under short sleeve Grateful Dead tie-dye, Adidas Oswegos, patchouli-soaked hemp necklace with a glass bead on it that some friends brought back from the Phish New Year's show in Miami. I wanted to look like a hippie. I wanted everyone to think "Woah, this kid is cool, he listens to Phish and the Grateful Dead." I wanted people to become fully aware of the fact that I liked to party, that I wasn't here to do any deep thinking or healing.

The two boys in the uniforms were current students. The men had appointed them as liaisons and little helpers to join me in my first few weeks at the Wilderness School. One of the boys is now dead. He was in a fatal car accident somewhere in California a few years after we left. I don't know much more than that, other than for a year, we were friends.

We all piled into a van and left the mansion. We drove for three hours to Eustis, Maine. I still had no idea what was going on. We spent the drive more or less trying to get to know one another—figuring out the stories that had landed us here.

It quickly became clear that we were heading to the middle of nowhere and having never been to Maine, we seemed to be going to the edge of existence. We arrived at a gate and continued down a long gravel road. At the end of the road was a small lodge. It seemed to be brand new. There was a barn and a few yurts. I had no idea what a yurt was, but I was about to live in one for three months.

The lodge was simple, but nice. It had a long table against the wall set with laptops and printers. There was a massive dining room table in the middle of the great room, a couch, and an industrial kitchen with a large range stove-top and an oven. Next to that was an industrial chest cooler. It was in the lodge that I taught myself to cook, something I'd love for the rest of my life. In a closet, lived a commercial washer and dryer, along with a safe where they would keep all our valuables and a stash of petty cash we'd use for activities.

Outside of the main lodge stood four shower stalls with cheap plastic shower curtains and a large bench. Next to these were a couple of single person bathrooms. The feeling of the grounds was similar to a sleep-away camp; all the amenities one needed were available.

Eventually there were two other instructors that emerged from another yurt. They worked in shifts of a week or two on and a week off, there were seven in rotation, and the two boys from the mansion were their assistants.

We were a five-minute walk down the road to Lake Flagstaff, which was more of a series of connected lakes no more than six feet deep at any point. It was beautiful. It may have been in the moment I first stood at the lake's edge that something, however small, shifted.

My time in the woods was the most productive time I would spend at boarding school. The instructors were crucial to me beginning to heal, even though I thought I was just surviving. They listened and they leveled with me. We spent the weekdays taking online classes that would accumulate credits in order for me to earn my high school diploma. On the weekends, we would go on long hikes through the Bigelow Mountain Range. I had never hiked in my life. On arrival, I was so out of shape but I quickly came into arguably the best physical shape of my life. I began to love nature and the simplicity and primal way of life I was living. Many of the hikes were silent. It was meant to be an exercise in meditation and reflection. Hiking twelve miles without talking was brutal at first, but I slowly began to enjoy it.

I was in the woods doing this for nine weeks, the entire summer. For fun, we would throw Frisbees, play music, swim in the lake, kayak, etc.—mostly things you'd enjoy at a normal summer camp. In contrast, the rest of our time was spent having insanely intense pseudo-therapy sessions with all the instructors, all of whom, were twenty-something year old recent college grads. I'd later learn they had been sold a pack of lies about working with troubled youth in the Maine wilderness. They had no idea what they were really getting themselves into. Many of the other kids were coming from seriously traumatic experiences and dysfunctional families that even some of the best professionals would have a hard time navigating.

One of the final tests we were asked to participate in was what they referred to as a "solo" which meant each student would be lead into the forest to a spot of their choosing and be challenged to be self-sustaining for a week. I was given rice, a small boiling pot, peanut butter, pita bread, and a bag of apples. I had a flint and needed to start a fire that would sustain me the entire time. I had a sleeping bag and a 6'x6' tarp with some para-cord to make a shelter. They also gave me a journal and a pencil to write and reflect on my time alone.

I was not pleased with the idea of being alone in the woods. I was angrier about being alone than the hardships that I would endure by being self-reliant. I spent most of the days lounging around and swimming in Lake Flagstaff. Eventually the boredom really sank in. Even pooping the normal way became dull, so I'd dig giant holes in the ground and climb to the very top of a pine tree and dangle my ass from a branch like an orangutan and poop from the tree into the holes twenty feet below. This was my entertainment. I also collected several boulders and wrote "Michael" with them some forty feet long. The instructors kept tabs on us from a distance by checking on a flag that we would put up a few times a day. If the flag wasn't reset, they'd come looking for us. I wonder if they ever saw me poop from the trees.

There was one night that I'll never forget toward the end of my stint in the woods. We were driving back from a three-day backpacking trip in the back of a massive black pickup fondly known as "Black Betty." My friend that I made during my time there named Donlee and I were in the backseat, exhausted and barely awake, but I remember Amy, an instructor who would later become a friend singing "Angel from Montgomery" by Bonnie Raitt to us as we fell soundly asleep. It was something about being sung to that calmed me beyond belief—I was so fragile then, and I really was trying to become better and stronger, but I was also being pushed and challenged to the edge of my very being. Every time I hear that song, I think of Amy and that night that we fell asleep to the sound of her voice.

At the end of the nine weeks I was sent from Eustis back to the main campus. I went through some serious healing and recovery that summer and it all came to a screeching halt once I was cast back into the general population of two hundred and fifty students I didn't know. Culture shock set in quickly.

I lived in a traditional dorm with about thirty-six other boys. We were forced to rotate roommates at monthly so that no one would be able to form strong enough bonds to get in cahoots with one another. This was the school's attempt at preventing any mutiny or bad behavior.

My first roommate was there because he had lost his entire family one day while his dad was driving their boat on Lake Champlain. His dad suffered an aneurism while driving and had lost control of the boat resulting in his mom and sister drowning from being knocked unconscious, and his dad dying from the aneurism. He woke up in the hospital with no family. I have no idea what ever happened to him.

My second roommate had alopecia from stress because his dad used to beat the shit out of him. He had cigarette burns all over his body, also a gift from his dad. I have no idea what ever happened to him.

Another roommate, who became a good friend, was there because his mom was hammered and she was driving his brother and his brother's friend home from a movie and she crashed the car and killed the little brother's friend. He's doing fine these days as a musician in New York.

Another roommate was a kid who also loved Phish and was a fantastic guitar player. I don't remember why he was there, but he's also living in New York as a musician and is close with the aforementioned friend.

Not all the kids were there because they were traumatized, there were plenty of garden variety spoiled rich brats who were products of parents that didn't give a shit about them and spent most of their money sending them to rehabs on tropical islands and overpriced shrinks.

I would say that the academic aspect of the school was about thirty percent of their focus while the other seventy was spent on what they referred to as "character education." They had a list of words which served as the foundation for everything that they were preaching. I remember "curiosity, concern, courage, leadership, and integrity" were a few of them. The aim of the school was to form the students into some utopic army of humans that would rule the world by being honest leaders with integrity and truth. They did their best at empowering dysfunctional teenagers to function in society as the elite, yet all they were doing was making us co-dependent on the school and their cult-like mantras.

If you were new, on your first day you were told that the next day you would have to sing a song acapella in front of the entire community. There would be an all school assembly in the performing arts center and you had to stand in front of everyone in this little taped off box in the center of the stage facing the bleachers and sing. This was meant to smash egos and put everyone on a level playing field. For whatever reason, I had no problem with this. I sang "Breathe" by Pink Floyd my first time. Most everyone else hated doing this. There were kids with serious attitude problems who thought they were hot-shit being forced to stand in front three-hundred people singing a song with no music. Kids would flat-out refuse to do this, which resulted in the entire audience being forced to do push-ups, planks, jumping jacks, or some other miserable physical workout until the student would give in. They would guilt people into singing, and sometimes this would go on for hours, sometimes postponing classes and meals.

Theft was a regular occurrence at the school. Kids would steal iPods, clothes, computers—anything of value. I remember on my eighteenth birthday, my grandma sent me a card with fifty bucks in it and I put it in my pants before wrestling practice only to find the cash gone after. I was furious, and heartbroken. They used the same technique to "wash out any dishonesty" whenever something like this happened. The entire school would go out to the lawn, rain or shine, and do physical workout punishments until someone fessed up. The culprit always showed their face after watching people suffer for long enough.

Another method for keeping order in place was threat of what they called "2/4" which meant twenty-four-hour isolation from the community. Any misstep in conduct would result in 2/4, which looked like this: You were sentenced to physical labor all day while the rest of the school went on without you. The population was forbidden to acknowledge you in any way—no eye contact, no talking, no nothing. You ate alone, worked alone, slept alone. You were shunned. Several times throughout the day you were forced to undergo intense physical workouts. Sometimes there would be garbage cans in place so you could puke into them after being physically exhausted. Periodically, staff would approach to ask how you were feeling and if your attitude was adjusting.

I spent a lot of time on 2/4 raking leaves, moving mulch, shoveling snow, etc. I never stole or really did anything more than mouth off and express my contempt for the way things were being run. This was more difficult for the staff to swallow because I was trying to incite mutiny and persuade others to open their eyes to what was really going on. Most of the time, I enjoyed 2/4—it was almost a vacation from the monotonous bullshit of the day-to-day. I liked being left alone. I didn't like going to class anyways and academically speaking, I wasn't learning anything.

Another ideology we were fed was what they referred to as "Brother's Keeper." It was meant to encourage students to hold peers accountable for their actions by essentially ratting them out. Let's say my friend Jimmy and I snuck out after hours and smoked a cigarette together behind the gym, and someone later caught Jimmy, but not me, and they found out that I was with him and didn't rat him out. Per the Brother's Keeper rule, I'd be in way more trouble than Jimmy for not holding him accountable. Again, another attempt at preventing bonds between students. Basically, the system made it impossible to make friends unless you found someone you really trusted. I had very few of these people.

The female population was seemingly much worse off than the males—their problems were more complex. A lot of them had been sexually assaulted, some had been subjected to prostitution. I knew that I didn't need to get mixed up in any of that. A lot of them were more than sexually available—there were mini-orgies in the woods and in the "serenity gazebo." It seemed that a lot of them knew that one way out of the school was to get knocked up.

I was still dating my high school girlfriend, who was a saint. She'd write me every day and send me care packages all the time. I'd wait for one of the two payphones inside the dorm every night to call her with a calling card that was provided to me by my mom. Really, this girlfriend is what got me through my time there. I never cheated on her while I was there. I knew that if I survived and pushed through, I could return to her and somehow resume life. Later, I'd fuck all that up, and to this day, never truly forgive myself for the way that I treated her. I loved her so much, but because of my substance abuse, anger, and depression, I tortured her for years. If you're reading this, I'm sorry.

My wrestling career at school was something positive. I had wrestled at my previous high school, and had made varsity as a freshman at my first high school only to be kicked off the team for smoking pot. It was the only sport I was good at. I ended my first and only season at boarding school with a record of 27/1 and I placed fourth in New England Sectionals. The one match I did lose was by technical fault. I never got pinned. I attribute this mostly to the fact that I was so pissed off all the time that trying to physically dominate someone else in a ring was the only way I could channel all my frustrations. I hated every second of it, but I was good at it.

I tried running cross country my first fall, but it didn't last long. Before the third race I decided to take a bunch of Ripped Fuel, a supplement that had ephedrine in it, and snorted some Adderall. I finished the race and shaved four minutes off my average time but felt like I was having a heart attack at the finish and was rushed to the hospital. If this wasn't ridiculous enough, upon returning from the hospital I was addressing my team and weaving together some bullshit apology about how I just wanted to "be a better runner" when an insect flew into my ear and I used the end of my glasses to try and dig it out only to rupture my eardrum and go right back to the same hospital.

My eighteenth birthday would have been a real bummer if it wasn't for a wilderness instructor named Joe, who, like Amy, is a great friend of mine today. In fact, she and her sister were the first visitors I had when I moved to Yosemite to write this book, and she is also the person who taught me most everything I know about backpacking and hiking.

She and her boyfriend at the time got special permission to take me off property to go see the movie *Garden State*. I timed it with my girlfriend so that we would see the movie at the same time that day and talk about it after. We did the same earlier that year with *The Notebook*. After the movie, I bought the soundtrack at a record store in Freeport and we listened to it as we drove along the coastal highway. We stopped at a farmer's market and bought apples and sampled a few different chilies and chowders. There wasn't anything extraordinarily special about that day other than the fact that I was with people who cared about me and knew I needed a breather from school. I suppose being stripped of most everything I thought I had, or deserved, or needed, forced me to appreciate the little things.

My final fond memory of boarding school was when my mom came to visit for a parent's weekend and we left the property for dinner. Leading up to this time, my relationship with my mom was beyond broken—I hated her. I hated her for loving me and trying to help me. She somehow found a restaurant called Le Garage on the Sheepscot River in Wiscasset. We took a table right by the window as the fog rolled in from the fall sea storms and enjoyed one of the best meals of my life. I had Lobster Newberg and clam chowder. I don't remember what she had. It was so nice enjoying a meal with my mom that night, away from school and all the pain it was causing me. I don't remember what we talked about, but I'll never forget that night.

While the systems and teachings at boarding school were meant to prepare us for the real world, what they were actually doing was molding us into people that would struggle greatly to survive in it. The structure, supports, and rigors of the school do not occur in the natural world, much less in modern American culture, and many kids bottomed out after they left—a handful died from overdoses, suicides, and car accidents.

In a way, it saved my life. I was a privileged kid from a good family, whether temporarily broken or not, that was caring and concerned enough to shell out a fortune to save me from myself. I am grateful for this. They used my grandfather's hard-earned money he made as a professional football player and coach for the Cleveland Browns to pay for the tuition. He was a Polish immigrant who suffered from grand mal epilepsy most of his life, who gave his heart and soul to my family. I wouldn't be where I am without him.

About eight years after leaving boarding school, a girl I was dating joined me on a road trip back to Maine. We stayed with my former instructor, Joe, in Portland for a few days and eventually made our way to the school. I wanted to revisit the campus—I wanted to see it with a new set of eyes. We pulled up and the place was empty, summer session had just ended. We walked around and I had hopes of finding fond memories, but I found none. I walked past the field where I puked and cried from forced exercise because someone stole, I walked past the medical clinic where I'd reluctantly swallow all the pills I was being fed, I walked into the performing arts center where we were forced to sing and have ridiculous school meetings where people would call one another out for "attitudes." We were maybe there an hour, then left without ceremony.

We then drove to an island to visit a good friend and his family. We went lobster fishing, ate acid on the beach, and saw one of the most amazing sunsets of my life. We attended a dance at the town hall, and I participated in a triathlon where I swam the third leg and came in third place. That was the last time I was in Maine.

Madison, Gary Lee, and Hospitality

Post boarding school, I spent some time in Cleveland working for a friend's father and taking classes at a local community college. The time was generally unproductive as I was partying and drinking a lot with kids that were younger than I was because all my friends had left for "real college." I missed the girl I dated while I was at boarding school, she had finally dumped me, so, me being me, I moved to Madison, WI where she was attending college. She didn't want me there, but it didn't stop me from trying.

I moved there with a kid I went to public high school with: we weren't friends then, but he would soon become one of my closest friends of all. He was attending CSU and wanted to get out of Cleveland. I told him that Madison was rad, so he came with, along with my dog, B.

It was there that I learned how to acquire an apartment, shop for groceries, set up an internet account, and be "on my own," whatever that meant at nineteen. We knew several other kids there, most of who were also from the same public high school.

I loved Madison immediately, perhaps because of the lakes, or the fun vibe, or maybe just because it wasn't Cleveland. I was starting over in a sense, even though I was only nineteen years old.

My first job was at a place on the capitol square that made Cornish pasties. I had no idea what these were at that point, but I didn't really care.

The shop was run and owned by a man named Myles and his best friend Ray. They got there early in the morning, baked, and prepped everything. I would show up in the afternoon to sell pies and close things up at the end of the night. It was a staple on the square, people loved their pasties, and they loved Myles.

An interesting thing about the homeless population that I came to know on the square was that they didn't really panhandle or beg. Almost all of them sat around and read all day. The public library was directly next to the pastry shop, and a library card cost less than five bucks. It was so funny to me to see these guys slumped on their backpacks in the sun all summer, reading and hanging out. They were almost all older men, older than say, sixty. Most of them slept at the shelter in the evenings and lived off social security checks.

I'd stand outside and shoot the shit with them after close and I learned about their lives, their pasts. Some were sad, some, who knows. I'd give them leftover coffee and the food that otherwise would have been thrown out at the end of each night.

One of the men was named Gary Lee. He was older than the rest of them, at least seventy if not more. He had a bum ankle and limped around. He was a Gulf War Veteran, if my memory serves, and had come from Florida.

Gary Lee was my favorite; in some ways, he reminded me of my grandfather on my mom's side. We'd sit and talk for hours. We'd smoke cigarettes and offer greetings to all the pretty girls that would walk by. He'd just tip his hat at them and say, "Ms." I loved it. They'd see that he was harmless and just smile back.

Eventually, I became comfortable with loaning Gary Lee cash. Most of the time it was because he was out of tobacco. He'd buy those huge drums and roll his own smokes and always paid me back, even though I didn't really expect him to. This went on for the duration of summer. Slowly, five bucks would become ten, ten would become twenty, etc. But he always paid me back.

I had learned that Gary Lee had grandchildren and a son and daughter living somewhere in Florida. He had a falling out with them for whatever reason and had been living in homeless shelters since. I was nineteen and had no business imparting advice on someone almost three times my age, but it always saddened me to think about the fact that this old man slept on a cot alone at night.

When winter arrives in Madison, many of the homeless head south, like birds. It's too cold to chance it on the streets, and if they didn't make it to the shelter in time, they'd run out of beds and be forced to a heated grate or freeze.

At this point, I had loaned something like thirty bucks to Gary Lee. A day went by, and there was no sign of him. A few more went by and I became concerned. I asked his buddies if they had seen him- no one had. At first, I was worried, and then I was a little pissed. I thought, "I guess I got ripped off. Oh well." That was that. I soon forgot about it.

A few months later I showed up for work one afternoon and Myles told me that a letter had arrived for me. No one would have sent me mail at work. It was postmarked from Tampa.

I opened the letter, and inside of it was a MoneyGram for $250 with a memo that read, "Dear Mike, I found my family. Thanks for being my friend, Gary Lee."

I've told this story so many times, and even writing it now I get choked up. I have no idea what happened to him. He might not even be alive at this point- he was my friend, though, and I'll never forget that.

When I wasn't partying and getting fat in Madison, the rest of my time was spent working toward my associate's degree in Hospitality and Tourism. At that age, I didn't know exactly what I wanted to do, but the job that I took after Myle's Teddywedger's was as a front desk associate at the Hilton Madison Monona Terrace.

I barely passed a drug test to get the job. I had been smoking weed all night before my initial paperwork session with the HR department, and when they asked me to take a saliva drug test, I panicked. I told the woman my mouth was dry, and asked if I could go to the drinking fountain. Much to my delight, she didn't notice that I brought the saliva swab with me, I soaked it with the water from the fountain and brought it right back. She applied it to the test strip, and voila! I passed. I wonder how things would have played out if I hadn't passed that test.

It was at the front desk of the Hilton that I learned to start taking care of people- I had a knack for it. I loved settling disputes and helping the most difficult guests. I also worked very closely with the Capitol Chophouse, the restaurant connected to the hotel. I would make dinner reservations for guests and promote the menu and extensive wine selection. The general manager was a guy named Josh. I'd sit at the front desk night after night and watch Josh schmooze guests and walk around in a fresh suit alongside beautiful female hostesses- I wanted this, I wanted to be a Josh. He started to notice my candor and professionalism with guests as well, and asked if I'd want to come and work for him in the restaurant. It was everything that I had wanted at that point: he was going to make me a lead host. I pictured myself wearing a suit every night, entertaining high-profile guests, pouring wine, etc.

The proper paperwork was submitted for my department transfer, and everything was lined up and ready to go, then I blew it. The head chef was set to marry one of the girls from room service and I was invited to the wedding. I attended the wedding which was held next door to the hotel at the Madison Club. I was honored to have been invited, and felt it was really my time to solidify myself among the restaurant staff that I had been slowly building a relationship with. I had been partying with two bridesmaids during the reception and they invited me back to their hotel room at the Hilton. A big no-no was "fraternizing with guests of the hotel as a hotel ambassador," but this slipped my mind that night. I had a slumber party of sorts with the bridesmaids and when I woke up the next day, I snuck out the fire stairwell, feeling on top of the world. When I showed up for my shift the next day, I was immediately called up to HR. The woman asked me if I had my front desk keys, and that's when I realized that they were already sitting on the desk in front of me. She said, "it's ok, we have them, two lovely girls dropped them off at the front desk this morning and told us that you had left them in their room, unfortunately, we have to terminate your employment." I can laugh at this now, but what a huge blow that was. Josh was sad, and probably disappointed, but everyone had a good laugh about it, at my expense of course.

Beyond promoting the Chophouse as a front desk associate, I was also responsible for knowing other restaurants around the city for guests who wanted to venture outside of the hotel for meals. I had dined at a restaurant across the street named Magnus with a friend and his parents a few months prior, and that particular dinner was probably the finest meal and experience I'd had up to that point.

Magnus was owned by one of four brothers who owned several other restaurants around Madison, all of which were extremely successful. I had been sending several guests to Magnus during the months before my termination and one night, Chris, the owner had come to the front desk and thanked me for all the business I had sent him, and told me if I ever wanted, I could come in for a free dinner. The day I got fired, I walked across the street and found Chris. I told him I had been fired, and that I was ready for my free meal.

This guy wined and dined me beyond belief. He prepared a chef's tasting menu that I'll never forget paired with several wines. I didn't have a clue what I was eating, but I knew then, that I wanted to learn as much as I could about food and wine, and that one day I would want a restaurant of my own. After dinner, he told me that a place called the Mansion Hill Inn was looking for someone to help open and run the place. It had recently been acquired by Trek Bicycle Corp and was undergoing a massive restoration. I applied immediately, and was hired.

The Mansion was stunning, and one of the most unique places I would ever work. Trek had bought it to house high profile employees and sponsored athletes like Lance Armstrong (I met him several times and always thought he was a douche bag). I also got to hang with Gary Fisher a bunch, and he was the man; we'd go drinking together at a tiki-bar named Jolly Bob's. I did a fine job at the Mansion, but eventually became too comfortable. I had the keys to the wine cellar in the basement, and had become accustomed to helping myself to anything and everything inside. One night, I invited a co-worker to join me for a few drinks after hours. The Mansion was vacant that night and my boss was out of town. We got hammered and slept in the nicest room of the Mansion, only to be found by a housekeeper in the morning who promptly called my boss, and once again, I was unemployed.

My next job was working at an art gallery that was owned by a former English professor from the University of Wisconsin. He was a quirky little Jewish guy who was highly intelligent, and also a very talented poker player. He had bought the art gallery to wash away his online poker earnings. We became close friends quickly, he taught me how to play nine ball and a lot about music. He took me to see Ryan Adams for my first time. Later, when I would return to Cleveland to pursue a Bachelors in English, I'd often call on him for help with essays and school papers.

Josh and I remained friends after I was fired from the Hilton. We'd cook together often, play disc golf, and he'd teach me more about wine and the finer things in life. We'd occupy the other establishments that were owned by Chris and his brothers. My favorite was Nattspil.

The place was an old Chinese laundromat that was behind Magnus. Chris' brother, Prentice, had imported some crazy slab of stone and built a wood fired pizza oven. They had a badass wine selection and great cocktails. The space itself was dimly lit, had a small DJ booth, and very limited seating. At the back of the restaurant was a small room with a Hobbit-esque oval door. Inside was a round table surrounded by tree stumps where people could convene privately, with the backdrop of a large mural of a Chinese woman smoking a massive spliff. The place was just cool. There was no sign on the door, no phone, no credit cards, and they served dim-sum style food.

Nattspil had a massive impact on how I viewed what a restaurant could be, and it would be stamped into my mind forever, even now when I think about the style of restaurant I hope to run one day. Chris and his brothers were doing things in restaurants that other cities and restaurateurs weren't even starting to think about. Farm-to-table started in Madison long before hipsters figured it out. I spent a lot, maybe too much time there eating, drinking, and listening to music. In fact, that's mostly what I did in Madison, period.

I made a lot of great friends in Madison, mostly hippie types who were in bands. I attended various concerts, themed parties, legendary farm parties that would last days fueled with weird drugs and weird music. I loved every second of it. I met my friends Katie and Brian, who were then a couple, and became extremely close with them. My time with them would become some of the more positive time I'd spend there. Madison is where I met Jeff, and several other people who would remain my friends for life. Native Wisconsinites are the best people I've ever met.

Eventually it began to dawn on me that my time there was coming to a close. I was surrounded by people who were working three jobs to pay for school when I had parents that were throwing money at me just to finish my associate's degree. I buckled down, finished my degree, and applied to John Carroll University back in Cleveland to pursue my bachelor's degree.

Those were some weird years. I ruined even the possibility of friendship with the girl I moved to Madison for, it took me four years to complete a two-year degree, I gained thirty pounds, got fired from two jobs, but learned a lot about food and restaurants, something I'd carry with me forever. Nine years later, I'd reconnect with Josh and move to Yosemite to work for him at a resort and write this book.

Coward in the Crabgrass

Summertime vacations in South Carolina with family and friends are some of my most precious memories. Riding golf carts around the island, swimming in the pool, eating epic seafood and playing pranks on my mom with my sisters fill the one week out of the year that I always look forward to. Some years ago, on one such trip, I made a different kind of memory. There are no pictures, journal entries, or postcards to document this experience, just this story, and the scars I keep on my heart.

Friends and I had met a group of locals at the bar one afternoon that invited us to some mansion for a party. They had spent the entire day at the beach club inviting anyone and everyone of all ages to come. We went on with our usual routine of day drinking, playing corn-hole and swimming. After dinner, with our respective families, I drove our golf cart to collect my friends from their house to pre-game at the pool bar. As the sun started to go down, I realized most everyone else was there, doing the same in preparation for the big house party. It was shaping up to be quite the event on this tiny island.

After a few drinks we hopped back on the golf cart and headed toward the mansion. It was indeed a massive home right on a bluff overlooking the ocean.

Music was blasting, and it was packed. A few people were standing outside smoking weed and cigarettes, and drinking from one of several kegs. Besides the beer, there was an entire wet bar next to the kitchen that was stocked with top shelf booze, enough to get a lot of people very drunk.

It turned out that no one was actually housesitting, as we'd been told by the locals, but rather one of the kids who was hired to clean and maintain properties on the island had a timetable of when the owners would be gone, and this particular home was scheduled to be empty for weeks. Of course, I didn't give a shit who the house belonged to or why it was available to us. There was tons of free booze, beautiful women running around in bathing suits, and the mansion had an infinity pool overlooking the ocean. I grabbed a cocktail, and went in.

As I scanned the crowd, I recognized the majority of the people there, they were adults that I'd seen sipping cocktails at the bar the past few days, questionably young teenagers, a few couples I'd gone to karaoke with and some guys I recognized from the golf course. I noticed one girl, looking very young and very drunk leaning up against a palmetto tree attempting to smoke a cigarette. She was wearing white shorts and a bathing suit top. No one seemed to be paying any attention to her and she didn't seem to be there with anyone. She could barely stand up.

I chatted with some people in the pool and then I went back inside to the bar to make another cocktail. I saw my friends playing beer pong and stood in the corner and decided to people-watch. The girl in the white shorts was inside now with a group of other girls her age. They were talking to a pretty ratty looking group of younger boys that I recognized from the surf shop. The boys were locals, and I'd seen them all week sliming on young girls at the pool and skating near the tennis courts. I watched as the girls flirted with them. It seemed normal with the exception of the one girl; she had a blank expression on her face and I could tell she was more than likely blacked out. A few of her friends went out to smoke with the boys but she stayed, swaying a little and spilling her drink in the kitchen. I thought to myself, "one of those kids is going to rape that girl."

I approached her and asked her how she was doing. With eyes not totally focused, she slurred, "I'm sooo drunk and these boys are sooo creepy and annoying and I just want to go home."

I agreed that the boys were creepy and asked who her rides were. She pointed to her friends outside. "They think they're cute. They're probably going to fuck them and leave me in the dust. I just want to go home. Also, the one dude won't leave me alone, the one with the blonde hair and tank top."

I looked over and saw the kid she was talking about. He looked like a shady little shit and he was glaring at the two of us as we chatted.

"I can see what you mean, I'd stay away from him if I were you."

I finished my drink and I went to the bar to fix another. My friends had me hop on the beer pong table and I lost track of the girl. I had intended on asking her if she wanted to hang close to us and grab a ride home with us, but she disappeared into the crowd.

I played a few rounds of beer pong with my friends and smoked some herb with some other people on the deck. Eventually, the friends I'd come with wanted to leave. I told them I wanted to find the drunk girl and see if she was ok or if she wanted a ride home. I looked around the party and didn't see her or any of her friends, or the boys they were talking with.

We grabbed a few beers for the road and made our way to the golf cart. I wanted to sit on the back so I could see the stars and enjoy my beer, so I had my buddy drive. When he started the cart, the brake lights casted a red glow over the crabgrass in the front yard and I noticed something moving about twenty feet away. The golf cart lurched forward. I held on, squinting in the dark, and I saw a girl sprawled out on her back in the grass, her white shorts in a small heap next to her, the ratty teenager on top of her.

I willed myself to yell, to jump off, to kick that fucking kid's head in and grab her limp body and wrap her up in a towel and take her someplace safe. I willed myself to be a hero, to save myself from the forever-guilt of allowing the world to have a place for pieces of shit like this...I locked eyes with the kid as we drove away, but he didn't stop, and I neither did I.

Life and Peas

I was leaving the Toyota dealership on the Bedford Auto Mile, it was gross and cold outside. I was already pissed because this was my second trip to Toyota that week. As I replayed the scene I'd just caused, screaming at the GM—which of course got me nowhere—I drove passed Planned Parenthood and noticed a mass of people gathered outside. There were picketers and protesters with tailgate pop-up tents and coolers of refreshments and bags of spent fast food. The people were your garden variety Jesus-Freaks, waving signs, chanting catchy pro-life slogans into their bullhorns.

I had been to this Planned Parenthood once before with my high school girlfriend. We had just begun having sex, and a condom slipped off (along with a million unborn Michael Murrays) inside of her. We freaked out. We didn't even know what the Plan B pill was, but we sure as hell didn't have a plan A. Nor did we have drivers' licenses. A friend who already had the inside scoop on dodging teen pregnancy offered to drive us there in his Range Rover that reeked of cigarettes. I remember it was gross out that day, and cold.

Sitting in the lobby surrounded by somber-looking patients and pamphlets about sexual education, vasectomies and adoption services, I felt my age—how young I was, out of place, and nervous. I went to pee and the bathroom had a sign warning people of becoming riddled with crabs. *Jesus.* My girlfriend was terrified, and I did my best, I suppose, to calm her. She filled out a bunch of paperwork, using fake names and addresses, and they called us into a private room.

Did you use protection?
How many days is her normal cycle?
Did you take an at-home pregnancy test yet?
Are you using the "pull-out" method?
Have you considered other forms of birth control?

We were fifteen. We didn't know what the fuck we were doing. We left with the pill, an assortment of literature and free condoms. The next few days were filled with pregnancy tests and worry, and eventually, it was over. There weren't any protesters that day, but I'm sure if there were I wouldn't have noticed.

Remembering that visit as I passed by, post-Toyota-incident, I became enraged. I pulled into the parking lot and approached a lady who was sitting under her tent in a camping chair with a few signs that had pictures of fetuses with Bible passages written underneath. I wondered how much time they had spent at Kinko's making these signs. I wondered what the people working at Kinko's thought about it.

The lady was friendly, but, already heated, I asked her if she would answer one question for me. I asked, "If you had a daughter, and she was raped, and became pregnant from the rape, would you keep the baby?"

She responded, with great conviction, "Why of course I would! How could anyone waste such a beautiful reminder of God's great work?"

Jesus.

Over the years my view of this whole thing, this place, would change a thousand times and a thousand ways, but one of the most potent influences on how I feel today was my experience with Olivia. My relationship with Olivia was more than likely the most meaningful one I had been in up to that time. I cared about her tremendously. She was four years younger than I was, and we met in a Shakespeare class at John Carroll. About eight months into our relationship, she texted me to say she was pregnant. I remember exactly where I was when I received that text; getting stoned and doing whip-its at a friend's house.

I snapped out of my nitrous and weed-filled stupor, told my friend what she had said, and I texted back, "I'll be home in ten."

I drove back to my mom's house and laid down in the hammock to call Olivia. When she answered, I could hear she was rattled. She said she missed her period and after becoming a little concerned, she and her friend went to get some pregnancy tests. I think she took three, and all were positive. The unique part of this scenario is that Olivia was twenty-one, and had a little sister that was turning two. Her mom and dad had an "oops" and decided to keep her. Olivia had a front row seat for what an un-aborted life could be. Her parents made it work, and I knew that Olivia was definitely considering that maybe we could work this out too.

I had just recently decided to take my academic career seriously. We were both broke, taking a full load of classes and I was living in a friend's carriage house taking care of his dogs as he traveled often for work. I had landed a job as a prep-chef at an upscale restaurant because I wanted to learn how to really cook. I lied to get my stage, and barely knew how to hold a knife correctly, but was a quick learner. Olivia and I would cook together often and watch indie-films. As per usual, I drank a lot, while Olivia would read. Most nights after she would fall asleep, I stayed up drinking and thinking about how much I wanted to finish school and get the hell out of Cleveland.

I said to Olivia, "I am not going to tell you what we should do about this, and I will stand by you no matter what, but I'm going to paint a picture for you: I have no money. My parents have a little, your parents already have a toddler to raise. We would more than likely have to move into my mom's basement, and you will be entering finals week pregnant. I will be graduating with a creative writing degree as a broke twenty-five-year-old expectant father."

I remember saying this, seeing this potential reality playing in my mind. I was chain-smoking as I rocked myself in the hammock. My mom came out and asked me what I was doing, I motioned that I was on the phone and it was important and she went back inside.

Olivia was crying. She said she had talked to her mom about it already, and that her mom had more or less told her the same thing: of course, if we had to we could make it work, but our lives would certainly be irreparably different.

The next morning we met up, and called Planned Parenthood. We attempted to make an appointment right away but they were either closed or booked out for a week. With no choice but to wait, I stumbled through finals week, feeling utterly lost. All the classic college student worries became just trivial bullshit as I tried desperately to focus on protecting Olivia and taking care of her however I could. I felt as helpless as I did at fifteen.

We finally secured an appointment and I drove Olivia there after school. When we arrived, there were a bunch of picketers outside with all their bullshit just waiting to remind us of our sins. I vividly remember one sign that read "Jesus hates you."

We went into an exam room that was decorated with a mobile made from condoms. Nothing like a bunch of rubbers dangling above your head as you prepare for your very first ultrasound. They gave Olivia a plain baby blue smock and some socks, which were multi-colored and had skulls and cross-bones on them. A large woman entered and I was immediately transported back to the exam room from a decade prior when she began to run through her list of familiar questions. We answered honestly this time, and took our verbal lashing—*we know…we know…we're fucking sorry, I'm sorry. I'm so fucking sorry.*

She lubed up this gray wand-like thing the size of an emulsion blender, put a rubber on it and began the examination. I sat next to Olivia and held her hand and we just stared at one another. After no time at all, the woman exclaimed jubilantly, "There it is. Looks like you're about five weeks in. It's the size of a small pea." A small pea. Fuck me. I've never looked at peas the same since. A pea, a little me, a little Olivia. The woman with the magic pea wand turned the screen to face us so we could see. Shit couldn't have been more real than it was in that moment.

Some of the details following this appointment are a little hazy, probably because I've spent years trying to forget them. What I do remember is both Olivia and I agreeing to abort the pea. The whole thing was so unbelievable to the both of us, it was like trying to rush through a construction zone while constantly getting stopped by flaggers and cops and obstacles on a road that, without truly realizing in that moment, is shredding your tires and grinding you down.

Luckily, we found out we were pregnant early enough that we were able to go with the medication method of abortion rather than the more invasive ones, but it was mandatory to have two separate appointments for the pills to be administered. The first appointment coincided with an English final that I couldn't miss. The idea of Olivia going back there and moving past the picketers alone made me sick. I asked a close friend who had had an abortion when she was younger if she would take Olivia. She did. Sitting in my final thinking of the two of them riding together, how hard it must have been, made me feel defeated, ashamed, and so sorry for her. I felt sorry for us.

The next appointment was for the second dose that would actually abort the pea, and would also be the most difficult. We timed it so that I wouldn't have to work that weekend, we would also be finished with finals. I turned my room into a sort of sanctuary. I bought some scented candles and cleaned the hell out of it. I brought out a bunch of blankets and ordered all of our favorite movies on-demand. I was so broke at the time that I actually had to borrow money for the meds—as if this whole ordeal wasn't shameful enough.

I held Olivia's nervous hand as she and I drove back to Planned Parenthood on Saturday morning. I don't remember there being much in the way of conversation; we were speechless and emotionally drained. Luckily, when we arrived that day, they had volunteers in the parking lot escorting patients from their cars to the building to shield them from the protesters. It felt less like a red-carpet escort than I'd hoped, and more like a public viewing party of our miserable walk-of-shame. But thank god for those volunteers. I may not have been able to hold Olivia and myself up without them.

We were seen immediately. The doctor gave Olivia a small paper cup with the second dose of meds and warned us of its harshness on the stomach, and more often than not, people puke it up. He gave her some Vicodin because it was also common that a great deal of pain in the form of cramps accompanies the process of forcing a miscarriage. We left and made it halfway home before I had to pull the car over because Olivia was puking out of the window. In this moment, we were in Hell. It was raining out and my girlfriend was puking up abortion meds on the side of Chagrin Blvd.

We turned around and headed back to the clinic, past the picketers again, got more meds, and waited for her stomach to settle. This time she put the pill under her tongue so it could dissolve slowly. We made it home and went straight to my room. We put on comfy clothes and waited. It didn't take long for things to start taking effect. For the next twelve hours Olivia went back and forth from the bed to the bathroom. We drifted in and out of sleep and binge-watched movies. When it was finally over, we slept for what felt like eternity.

This experience would be just one of many catalysts that undoubtedly unraveled our relationship, but it was the first, and the biggest. After the abortion, I started drinking harder. In the coming months, an onslaught of unforeseen events derailed me even further. My friend was killed in a car accident, the professor whose class I had met Olivia in died suddenly at 44, I got kicked out of the carriage house because my friend's dog ate weed food I'd baked, and I found out one of my oldest and closest friends was shooting heroin. I simply couldn't take care of her anymore. I couldn't take care of myself.

When I reached out to Olivia about publishing this essay, she not only granted me permission, but offered to share her memories of the experience:

Dear Michael,

We met at your parent's house. I sat across your lap and cried. You held me like a baby—I remember thinking that.

I was supposed to eat first so I scarfed down a PB&J. I puked it up in huge chunks on the side of the road.

I think we had to get a Vicodin prescription filled because I remember being at CVS feeling so sick and having to buy pads.

I remember standing up and blood dripping onto your L.L. Bean socks that I stole because I was embarrassed. They're still the comfiest pair I own. I put them on yesterday after my rat died.

Our friend who drove me to the appointment you couldn't' make wanted to stop at Starbucks after and I felt like I needed to do something for her to thank her for taking me. She wouldn't even let me pay for her coffee.

I took the tests after a catering job so it was late, like midnight. I bought the tests at Walmart.

I woke my mom up crying and laid next to her and my sister—she asked me if you loved me and if you told me that.

-- Olivia

The stigma associated with facilities that offer abortion services forces us to keep secrets, live in "moral failure" alone, as if it was our own family, friends, and all the world standing outside holding those heinous signs, or worse. Beyond the fact that abortions are only a small fraction of the services that

Planned Parenthood provides, there aren't "high class" or "Platinum Member" Planned Parenthoods. Whether you're a socialite from the suburbs, a teenager from the ghetto, or just a dude struggling to figure it all out, we're all going to the same place. The waiting room is strangely akin to the Kentucky Derby—all walks of life are represented there, and they're all there for the same reason. The difference is that no one is drinking mint juleps or wearing fancy hats. At Planned Parenthood, we are hiding beneath oversized hoodies, usually alone, drowning in our shame.

I've donated to Planned Parenthood annually since our abortion, and will continue to do so for the rest of my life.

On Opiates

I was sixteen when I attended my first funeral for an opiate overdose. Since then, I've known dozens of people, some of them very close friends, who have died from opiates. I've gone to several of their funerals, and for a while, it got to a point where it felt like there was one every other month. How I never got into these drugs is beyond me. Honestly, they scared me.

I accidentally snorted an OxyContin once. I was with some friends at a bar in Madison, WI when one of them told me there was a present for me under the flower pot in the bathroom. I found a line of powder underneath it and snorted it thinking it was cocaine (yes, sadly this was normal for me). It wasn't coke, it was a thirty-milligram OxyContin, and it sent me backwards into the wall of the bathroom. I puked almost immediately and then I felt like I was having a strange, unwarranted orgasm minutes later. It was an uncomfortable sort of high; I loved it, but it scared me. I felt dirty. All I kept thinking was: _Nothing should feel this good,_ and _I could do this every day and no one would have a clue._ Both were terrifying realizations. I still had my motor functions, and in a way, I felt more confident than ever. I never did it again. It felt wrong. I felt like I had opened a door that I shouldn't have and that I had some dirty secret that made me feel sad. I didn't enjoy it.

I vaguely remember when OxyContin hit the market in the late 90's. I watched a 20/20 special where it was posed as a "miracle drug." People who had chronic pain such as burn victims or terminally ill cancer patients were finally calm and painless. Of course they felt great. They were being given synthetic heroin! Since then, it's become out of control.

As of March 2018, more than 115 people die from opiate related deaths in the United States every day. This is an alarming and disgusting statistic. It certainly feels like a large percentage of that number must be represented by the area where I grew up, in Northeast Ohio. I'm not going to mention details of people I've known that have died or struggled with these drugs, but I will say that I have spent years heartbroken over one friend that should be dead, but somehow isn't. Everyone was in denial about how truly bad this person's issues were, and for years I felt I was the only person who truly knew the gravity of the situation. I was ridiculed by people for wanting to call this person out and help them, but lies, vanity, and denial got in my way. I love this person with everything that I have, and I hope somewhere inside of them, they know this, but just the other day I heard they were still using.

```
Loving you is like watching you tie a
    noose above your head
and slowly step on to the chair beneath
    you with toddler like imbalance.

You reach for the rope with both hands,
the chair shakes,
and eventually you'll get it.

My arms are tied behind my back.
I'm forced to watch
and wait.
```

For me, this poem I wrote about this person accurately describes the torture and powerlessness that accompanies knowing someone who struggles with an opiate addiction. There is virtually nothing you can do. I know this now, and in the saddest way possible, have accepted it. I have pre-written dozens of eulogies for this person as some form or preparation or catharsis, I have pictured my friends and I carrying their casket down the aisle, and imagined us holding each other and crying. I have felt the pain already. I have, in a way, prepared for them to die.

Misinformed people resort to unfounded, idealistic excuses to blame for the opiate epidemic. They blame gateway drugs, black drug dealers from the inner city, not being involved in sports or regular activities, whatever...if this country wants people to stop dying from opiates, they need to go after the government and the pharmaceutical companies and corporations that are manufacturing the litany of opiate-based pain killers that are widely available. Between the doctors who prescribe with a simple swipe of their pen, nurses who steal or sell them, and the pharmacists that regularly fill the scripts when they know they shouldn't, they're all complicit and have blood on their hands. The most deplorable part is the government's answer; providing (and making a fortune from) synthetic opiate-based meds like Suboxone or Methadone, which only shift the addiction focus away from the pills originally handed out like Skittles that created dependence in the first place. It is like fighting fire with gasoline, and getting paid millions to do it with seemingly clean hands. It's fucked.

I understand heroin enough to know that once you've gotten into it, it's a monkey on your back for the rest of your life—it consumes your soul. It turns you into a liar, a thief, and a faint shadow of whoever you once were, and that's only if it doesn't kill you. It's terrifying how long the human body can survive on it once it becomes dependent. My mom often works with "heroin babies" in the NICU and tells me how horrifying it is to see a premature newborn writhing in opiate withdrawals the second they are born. It is *almost* impossible to stop, but it can be done. I've seen it happen. I have a friend who kicked opiates by flying to San Diego and driving across the Mexican border to participate in Ibogaine treatments. If you don't know what this is, look it up. Of course, it's not approved by the FDA because it actually helps, and the government hasn't figured out how to make money from it yet. Why would the government allow something that actually helps when they can sell and control both the poison and the antidote exclusively, banning anyone else from getting in on the profits? It is a monopoly.

Since my friend kicked opiates, he has flown his former dealer to Mexico, got him clean, and did the same with his two brothers.

I don't have an answer for this. The best I can come up with is this: the fish stinks from the head. These drugs are being pushed onto the streets by the government and drug dealers wearing designer suits and lab coats. Wake up.

Grad School

September 12th, 2014

I am not sure what I am doing right now. I feel I am slowly beginning to understand exactly why I am here: to write. It has been an intensely odd and awkward journey to this very introductory statement. The first workshop scared me quite a bit because I finally realized that I am in the big leagues now. I feel extremely inadequate because some of the comments during workshop were things I would have never thought of. I feel like everyone else is on a much higher plane of thinking than I am right now and it is scaring me. I see poems everywhere…in a walk to the coffee shop, or even unlocking my bike and seeing garbage on the ground. My problem now is getting these thoughts down on paper. At the moment, I follow a certain "recipe" for writing poems, and I hope to have that recipe tossed aside for a while. I am here to get lost with my writing, and hopefully arrive at a newer, more intelligent way of thinking and writing. I want my poetry to convey the way that I see the world. I tend to write about the absurdity of things, or rather my perception of what I deem to be absurd. This has worked for me in the past, but it also perpetuates my negative outlook on the world, and further my negative perception of myself. When I read my poetry sample writing submitted for this program, I hadn't read a lot of that selection of work in a while. Reading them, I began to cry. I felt that a lot of the poems were too sad and almost served as a reminder of things I would rather not think about anymore. So, I would like to move past this way of writing and thinking. The last thing I need right now is to slip into depression again.

Some of the most important influences on my poetry are tiny moments that would otherwise go unnoticed to most people. I do not have any particular people or places that spark interest. I just try to stop during moments in life that evoke rapture, happiness, anger, sadness, lust, and notice them for longer than other people might. I like imagining what someone's life must be like, and adding my own details or presumptions into the mix. I also turn to watching the news a lot for inspiration- but this generally leads to the depression previously mentioned.

My revision process varies, when writing on my own, my normal routine is to write down an idea, and leave it. I wait a while and then return to an idea and if I feel it's worth writing about then I will write down every little detail that I can think about relating to the idea. I almost always try to write my poems as stories. I write the story down with no regard for any traditional grammar, just a blob on a page. Then I begin subtracting lines and words that are unnecessary or ambiguous. Next, I focus on making the small ideas within the original idea sound more interesting.

I have never been interested in trying to make my writing overly complicated or mysterious, which brings about another factor; I always think about how the poem will sound while being read aloud. I practice reading the poem in my head and that is usually how I decide where line breaks and such will go. I attempt to have most poems flow smoothly as if they were being heard rather than read, and almost always like to have a turn of events at the end of each poem.

I feel that I admire certain writers more for their choice of subject matter rather than the way their poems are written. Dorianne Laux, Bob Hicok, Erica Dawson, and Simon Armitage are all poets who's work I enjoy and try to emulate because much of their work is very prosaic. I enjoy how many of these writers will pick a certain object like a kite, or lips in a rearview mirror, or a stapler and write about their own relationship to the object, or use the object to explain or show something they find beautiful or ugly. Erica Dawson's "The Absence That Was The Tree" is an example of taking the image of a hole in the ground, something we see all the time, and explaining how she sees it. The poem shows that in the absence of the tree, there are also many other things absent, like birds, leaves, swings, tree houses, memories, etc. This is how I like to write, and this is a move that I covet.

For me, poetry is a form of expression that has become a way that I can alleviate some of the pressures and feelings of anxiety that I have. I believe a lot of things about poetry. I believe that indeed, poetry is the mathematics of language, but has no boundaries or rules like math. Poetry can be anything, and anything can be a poem. Sitting in line at the DMV waiting to get new tags for your car can be turned into a poem. Poems don't need to be written on paper, and some poems don't need to be written down at all. I believe that it takes a certain individual to understand poetry, and that it is not for everyone. I do not believe that poetry can change the world, or even make it a more enjoyable place to be, but sometimes when I write I feel catharsis and I feel more comfortable, even if only for a moment.

I think the most helpful thing I can take away from workshop is brutal honesty. I am not confident in my work a lot of times and I am genuinely interested in what people have to offer in the way of criticism. Sometimes brutal honesty can hurt, but only if one takes it personally, and I don't think taking things personally in workshop is a great thing. However, if a piece of criticism doesn't resonate well with me, perhaps it will give me the drive or fire that I need to write something much better than I had intended.

I would like you to know that I am terrified about this process. That is all I have to say about that at this time.

Other creative activities that I engage in would be teaching yoga, and cooking. I find a lot of similarities between cooking and writing. It's can be a highly personal experience to create something that changes others. Working extremely hard to prepare a meal for someone and seeing the results whether good or bad is exciting to me. Besides the general rules for cooking, it's entirely up to the chef to decide what is going to happen. Ingredients are like words, and they can be subbed in and out of whatever is being prepared. Sometimes ingredients add excellent flavor and variety; sometimes they don't. I find the same satisfaction in preparing a good meal for someone in the same way I find it when someone compliments a poem I have written. Often times in cooking, less is more; sometimes this is true with poetry, sometimes not.

I also appreciate live music. Last night I went to see Ryan Adams at the concert hall near campus and had a pretty profound experience. I went to the show alone and was already feeling a little insecure. I sat at the very top, alone and began thinking about the fact that Adams dropped out of high school because he enjoyed writing short stories on his grandmother's typewriter more than sitting in a classroom. He was obsessed with Poe, Henry Miller, and Kerouac. He is an excellent writer, storyteller, and has a stunning voice with unparalleled range for a forty-year-old male. Tens of thousands of people from all ages paid $70 to see him play for an hour and a half last night. I find power and inspiration in this. This guy never graduated from high school. I have all the tools and talents I need to write, I just need to find my voice, and play with my range. I would say, in so many words, that that is what I think I am doing.

September 11th, 2015

"This has worked for me in the past, but it also perpetuates my negative outlook on the world, and further, my negative perception of myself."

"So, I would like to move past this way of writing and thinking. The last thing I need right now is to slip into depression again."

Hm. Well, saying things have improved would be a lie, so I won't. Re-reading my intro statement from last year has me feeling...who knows. Honestly, I haven't written since the last workshop this past spring. Not a word. My summer sucked. I spent half of it thinking I was in love and spent the other half drinking myself into a stupor and surfing by myself every day, oh, and working of course. I estimate I worked over thirty weddings this summer, and let me tell you, bartending at weddings after your heart gets broken is enough to drive anyone insane. On that subject, let's talk about how I am pretty sure I've lost my mind. I am depressed, more than I have been in a long time. Yes, a girl is responsible for a lot of it, but I won't give her the credit she deserves. I am so insecure that I applied for a grad program so that I could prove to everyone I grew up around that I wasn't a fuckup. I thought I wanted to be a college professor and live in a cool college town and get to blow student's minds with amazing literature and I want none of that anymore. I don't even want to teach high school. I have half-heartedly applied for a few internships or whatever mostly because I want to save money. Oh, let's talk about money, about how I'll be broke when I'm done with this venture, and I don't think there's anything cool or romantic about being single, twenty-nine, and broke with a writing degree. What a goddamn nightmare my brain is right now. I'm sad. I hate so many of the inhabitants of Portland that I honestly think I've developed some type of subconscious numbing mechanism that allows me to see the nonsense that I see and hear without even feeling anything but apathy about it anymore. I feel like there must have been some broadcast that told every socially awkward outcast who didn't fit in where they grew up and told them all to move to Portland. The shit people get away with here is lunacy. I know that I feel this way because I grew up in Cleveland. I know that I sound like an asshole, but when I get into an altercation with a fat lesbian because I held the door for her and she asks me if I would have done the same thing if she were a man, thus trying to insert some feminist lesson into my life, that's where I draw the line. I'm sorry I grew up in a family that taught me to hold doors for everyone. Try pulling that shit where I grew up and see where it gets you. No one gives a shit about your feelings.

Work—don't be an asshole and relax. I'm so tired of hearing everyone's unsolicited opinions about every little goddamn thing. No one cares. I've also never met more lazy humans in my life. People say Portland is progressive. My ass. Yesterday I stepped on a bloody syringe outside my car door. Later, I got to work and had to call 911 because some homeless piece of shit overdosed while sitting at one of the picnic tables out back. Then tonight when I got to work there was a pile of human shit on the ground I had to clean up. Kill me now. People try to argue that "there's a large mental health epidemic, that's why there are so many homeless" or "transients" or whatever euphemism they come up with. No, actually it's just what happens when people use meth and bath salts. The tolerance that I see around here is deplorable. Why am I depressed? Because I know how good I have it and it kills me. I am a selfish little baby who can't get over himself and it just doesn't ever seem to end. I am sitting around bitching about not wanting to go back to school to sit in a room with no windows and spout ambiguous who knows what and two years ago I dedicated a year of my life to get into grad school. I spent thousands of dollars and countless hours toiling away in libraries and bars and here I sit, bitching. I know there are thousands of people who would kill to sit where I am, trust me; I used to be one of these people. Wow, I'm really on a roll right now. I'm sad all the goddamn time. I miss my dog. I don't miss Cleveland per se, but I miss Cleveland. It would take too long to explain this, so I'll just leave it be. I'll take a moment to talk about things that make me happy. I left a job that I hated, actually I got fired for taking the week of 4th of July off to go screw around at the coast with my friend Pete. That was a great time. When I got back I walked into a restaurant that I would hang out at all the time (because of how impressed I was with everything they did) and I asked them for a job. Straight up. I said, "I know you don't give a shit but I know a lot about working in restaurants and I want to work here and I am prepared to show you that I know what I'm talking about." They told me to go home and come back at five for a working interview. I got the job two days later and thank god. It's been the only distraction I have lately and I love everyone I work with.

I love surfing. I taught myself how to surf this summer. After my miserable ex-girlfriend left me sobbing on my front porch to the point of puking I decided that I was going to learn how to surf. I started waking up every day at the crack of dawn and driving out to the coast and renting gear. Three months later I am a confident surfer. I own my own gear, and learned by watching YouTube videos. The sad thing is that I started doing this because I secretly hoped I would die every time I went out. The number one rule of surfing is never go alone. I estimate I have surfed maybe 30 times and I have only gone with other people twice. I like the way it feels to get tossed around like a ragdoll in the waves. The ocean doesn't give a shit about me. I am insignificant when I am in the water and I am fine with that. No one and no thing has ever fought the ocean and won. One day, a few weeks ago I was out and saw an entire pod of orcas 50 yards from me. God damn, life can truly be so incredible sometimes. I also woke up one morning still drunk from the night before and thought it would be a great idea to go skydiving. I went alone. No video, no Instagram or Facebook photos, just me jumping from an airplane because I wanted to see what it would be like to almost die. Well, it's pretty intense I'll say that much. The only thought I had when I landed was "well, nothing else is ever going to cool anymore." My friend Jeff is moving to California from Wisconsin. I've never met anyone like this guy. He's my best friend ever. I don't know sadness when I'm around him, I don't worry about anything, ever. We lived together in Madison for about a year, but we were inseparable. If all works out, he'll be up here really soon, and I can't wait. In my first intro, I talk about watching the news for inspiration and whatnot. Jesus. If I watched the news now I think I'd be even worse off than I am now, shootings all the time, racist cops, hurricanes...these jokers on the political campaign trail making a theatrical mockery of whatever tradition this bullshit country was founded on. Who cares about Donald Trump? Not me.

I'm going to plow through the rest of this program and stop censoring what I have to say. It's not doing anyone any good. I am a good writer. I have no idea what I'll do for my thesis, but it'll come to me. When I am done with this program I will write a book, maybe a few books...memoirs. I will feel complete and accomplished. I owe it to myself and to the people who have supported this endeavor of mine. It's my destiny. I've crammed lifetimes of experience into 29 years and if Cheryl Strayed can write a book about her struggles (not even a very well written book in my opinion) and make millions and not have to worry about shit ever again, then I can do it too.

Finish strong: Write a book, build a prison somewhere in the woods or on the coast. Surf, cook, write.

Calling All Idiots

Did you not fit in well as a kid? Picked on? Nerdy type?

Have you always wanted to shave half your head and wear adult sized onesies to a fine dining restaurant?

Does being 42 years old and long boarding to your barista job with your dog in a book bag interest you?

Do you want to quit life and openly shoot heroin and smoke crack right next to joggers and cyclists along the Willamette?

Would you fancy taking a shit on the sidewalk outside Nordstrom?

Do you get off on random political discussions in which you feel totally justified all the time?

Are you a fan of American Spirits, E-Cigarettes, openly smoking vape pens in public?

Are you sick and tired of being judged?

Do you feel the need to flaunt the fact that you're gay or bisexual or transgender?

Would you like to shop at Whole Foods or New Seasons Market with government Food Stamps?

Are you afraid of black people and do you confuse culture with trends?

Do you think you're a genius because you can make a craft cocktail?

Do you think you have celiac disease?

Come to Portland!

Everyone I Love is Drunk

Everyone I love is drunk and they're packed in a room toward the back right corner of my brain causing a raucous about whether or not I'm ever going to come home or if I'm flying to Newport for Nicole's wedding and little salad tongs that look like leaves and whether or not the school district where they might buy a house is safe and if so and so is going to have a gluten-free option and dairy alternative at this year's Rainbow Babies Hunter Jumper Classic and if I heard that so and so got arrested and everyone I love is drunk on playing paddle tennis and putting up pictures of the type of wine they're drinking tonight and they're drunk on going to CAVS games with matching outfits and taking pictures of the court so I can see how nice their seats are and they're drunk on riding horses and shooting skeet and fly fishing and backcountry skiing and they're drunk on putting up "black lives matter" signs in their massive front yards and they're drunk on mailboxes custom made, to scale, that look just like their homes and

everyone I love is drunk on this new cleanse package that Whole Foods just released and changing their Facebook profile pictures to the rainbow setting and the newest sour that Ecliptic Brewery released that was barrel aged in old pinot noir casks and this new restaurant that only serves various preparations of mussels and how the Everett House Healing Spa has complimentary shampoos that are made of 100% locally sourced material including the plastic that the bottles are made of and everyone I love is drunk on this new yoga studio where one can get a colonic, a smoked salmon Niçoise salad, home- made kombucha, and these camouflage yoga pants (which are also made of recycled plastic) and they're drunk about all the food carts closing downtown and the giant earthquake that will supposedly decimate the coast and they're drunk on Andrew Bird playing at the Schnitz and everyone I love is piss-wasted on Facebook and feeling a little artsy on Instagram and a little blacked out on Tinder pictures of themselves doing handstands in front of Haystack rock or a carefully taken picture of themselves with their dog overlooking the gorge and the rain keeps raining and the lady who sleeps in the bushes outside my restaurant is still sleeping and the 17 bus is still 17bussing and the old guys at yoga that smell are still the old guys at yoga that smell and my roommate keeps leaving the door unlocked and Donald Trump is definitely still Donald Trumping and the dust on the lampshade keeps collecting and my dog is getting older and everyone I love is loving.

Spring Break

I stood barefoot, shaking, with Oberlin College mesh shorts and a Gap hoodie that still had bloody coke snot all over it. It was something like 5:30 in the morning and it was 47 degrees out. I couldn't feel the frost beneath my numb feet, and I couldn't feel my right hand as it held a pint glass of gin and grapefruit juice. I stood, waiting for my next Klonopin to take me back to the couch where I would lie and continue trying to not feel. As I stood on that deck, my brain felt as though someone had taken a tourniquet and tied it off—preventing anything from expanding or collapsing. It was mid-March, and it was quiet. I kept thinking about how the conversation with Fritz had gone the night before...

"Your mom and your sisters and I love you very much," he said over the phone, so far away.

I continued to shake and cry and my tears froze to my cheeks. I was so drunk I was sober. I kept getting nosebleeds every time I sniffled but I didn't care. I wanted a terminal cancer prognosis. I wanted a frozen branch to fall and crush me. I wanted to wander through Glacier National Park until I froze to death or was eaten by a grizzly, ripped to pieces. I wanted to be taken out of the game, benched for life. I wanted sleep. I wanted to die because I wanted to die. I returned to the couch after making another drink and laid down staring out the window.

When I woke, I showered. I felt the hot water run over me and I blew my nose until I could form a decent clot with some toilet paper. Dagmara had stocked my bathroom with organic shampoos, soaps, and conditioners, and had told me I could stay as long as I liked. Dag is my best friend Bacon's ex-girlfriend. She's from the west side of Cleveland and she recently moved to a four-bedroom mansion nestled right in the middle of Whitefish, Montana. She lives alone with three dogs and is more or less semi-retired after settling a sizeable law-suit from a car accident. She works part-time from home in the search engine optimization field. There's nothing sexual between us whatsoever, which is probably why we get along so well. It takes about an hour just for her to get out the door to go grab a cup of coffee because the dog's needs come before anything else in Dag's world. I know this, and have accepted it.

I heard the sliding door open, Dagmara popped her head out and said, "Hey Murray" as she let the dogs out. The dogs chased a deer at the perimeter of the fence. They did their morning ritual and returned to the sliding door where I let them in. At the end of the road was Whitefish Lake State Park, and the sun was slowly beginning to rise.

I knew I couldn't stay here forever. I hadn't talked to the rest of my family yet, and I knew Megan would be the most difficult one to speak with. I took an Adderall and put my long-johns and ski pants on along with a fresh base layer and went into the kitchen. I began pounding as much water as I could along with lemon juice and apple cider vinegar. I took a few protein bars and went out through the garage to warm up my car. Dagmara had returned to sleep with the dogs, so I wrote her a note.

"Went skiing, give me a jingle when you wake – Murray"

As I pulled out of the driveway, I remembered it was St. Patrick's Day. I opened Spotify on my phone and found the album *Reunion* by The Clancy Brothers. This, I thought to myself, is an album only the true Irish would know, and it's an album I've been listening to since I was a child. I'd wake up mornings on St. Patty's Day and my mom would be in the kitchen blasting "Carrickfergus," "Tim Finnegan's Wake," and "Will Ye Go Lassie Go" at the loudest of decibels, singing in her fake Irish brogue. The house would smell of corned beef and cabbage that had been braised in Guinness and brown sugar along with carrots and red-skin potatoes. My sisters would be sleeping and my mom would be in full regalia with her green and white striped socks, her leprechaun apron, four-leaf clover hat, and a long sleeve St. Malachy's 1997 5K shirt.

I pointed the car toward the mountains and began driving. I chose to listen to "Finnegan's Wake" first,

117

knowing that I would cry- I just wanted to get it over with. For whatever reason, the chorus of this particular version of the song always resonated with me- the stomping of the musician's feet, the crowd clapping, the force of their voices would wash over me and give me the chills.

My crying began to subside as "Mountain Dew" played. I pulled into the parking lot and it was snowing heavily. The place was almost empty. I knew I would have first chair and fresh tracks for most of the day. I geared up and hiked to the main lift. In line, I was about fifteen rows back from the lift operators. Those who were there were wearing green and drinking PBR's. A few people tried to talk to me but I motioned with my hands toward my helmet that I was wearing headphones and couldn't hear them.

Oh, the summertime is coming, and trees are sweetly blooming, and the wild mountain thyme grows around the blooming heather, will ye go lassie go..

It was amazing how much snow had fallen overnight. It was the thick, dry fluffy stuff that sits softly on the earth. When you move over it, it feels like you're floating on a cloud. I was extremely careful, as the terrain was much more difficult than what I had become used to skiing on the east coast during my younger days. Even in all of my misery, I was still scared to hurt myself skiing. Mere hours before this moment I wanted to die. Go figure.

I went to the backside of the western bowl where I knew there would be even fewer people and made my way up and down the various runs. I could see all the way to the gates of eastern and western Glacier National Park from the top of the Hellroaring lift. I tried taking pictures but it really was impossible to capture such magnificence with a smart phone.

I skied until about noon, and went into the base lodge to have an Irish coffee. I knew no one. Most everyone was in high spirits inside the bar. Bluegrass was playing, which is as about as close to Irish music as the bartender could find, I suppose. He had a small dropper inside a rocks glass filled with green food coloring he was adding to the beers if people wanted it. I stared out the window. How beautifully lonely I felt. I skied a few more runs and when my legs began to weaken I quit and drove back to Dagmara's.

When I arrived, she was working in the kitchen at a stand-up desk she had ordered for lumbar support or something weird.

"How're you doing, Murray? How was the mountain?"

"Great, I just listened to Irish music and hot-lapped the back bowl, the place was near empty. I went twenty-two minutes without seeing a single person, I timed it."

"Wow. What's your plan for the rest of the day? Have you slept yet?"

"Not really, I'm gonna try to now."

119

I went into the room she had set up for me and fell onto the bed. Almost immediately, my head started spinning and I started shaking. I jumped up and went back into the great room to lie down on the couch near Dag.

"I can't be alone in a room by myself right now, my head's spinning. I'm just gonna crash here for a bit if it's cool..."

"Of course, Murray. Cuddle with the dogs."

I drifted in and out of something like a hangover, a day-drunk, and a trance of earthshakingly depressing thoughts for the better part of the afternoon before I decided that enough was enough. "How am I going to move on from this?" I thought. I couldn't imagine returning to Portland and facing the mess that I had created. I didn't care about school. I didn't care that I had already told work I wasn't coming back only to beg for my job back less than twelve hours later. After attempting to explain what happened to Bacon, he told me "people rarely remember how fucked-up someone gets in life, what they remember is how one crawls out of it." I suppose this was true.

I took another shower and got ready to head into downtown Whitefish. I didn't have any Irish-looking clothes, so I threw on a flannel, some boots and a vest. Dag dropped me off at Casey's Irish pub downtown and I mingled with the locals for a while. I was extremely homesick. There was an Irish band playing music upstairs and much to my delight, they were incredible. It was a group of older guys from Kalispell and apparently they had been playing St. Patty's Day annually. I felt somewhat at home while listening to them play, and even more to my delight, they were playing the very songs I had been listening to that morning. There was a young couple in the audience with their son, who was about three years old. Something about seeing this family resonated with me as I tried to remember what it must have been like back when my parents were still together, and how they surely brought me to Irish bars to hear music on Patty's Day. I thought about being that young and not having a clue what life had in store. How pure and innocent those days were—the blissful ignorance of childhood.

Megan is my younger sister by five years. We talk at least every other day usually for about an hour. She used to work a management level position at Nordstrom but eventually ran into a snag because of a boss that had it out for her, and because she is hotheaded like me, she quit. Now she works at one of the two local watering holes in our part of Cleveland. We know the owner well and have for most of our lives. He's your garden-variety drunk Irishman who smokes two packs of Marlboros a day and has every bit of his pride tied into this little bar of his. They have a great burger that comes on an English muffin with bacon and blue cheese. Every now and then the owner will get shitfaced and lock the doors so patrons can smoke inside. He'll dance on the bar to some Rolling Stones and buy everyone a round. People feel special. Megan gets to serve all of the locals who practically live there, the kind of people who start their day off by reading the morning paper that is already laid out for them at their designated bar spot along with a cocktail. They talk Cleveland sports and start cranking Dewar's and rocks at 11 a.m.

I left Casey's and bummed a smoke off a guy on the corner and decided to call Megan. After three rings, she picked up.

"Hey bud, how are ya?"

"Hanging in there, are you busy?"

"Nope, just finished working this shit-show holiday. Are you ready to talk?"

"Yup," I said with a feeling of surrender.

"It's good to hear your voice, obviously everyone is worried as shit and making their own predictions as to what happened with you guys out there. I was at a fundraiser with Griz when I got the call about you missing. What happened bud?"

As I began to try and formulate my response, some drunk girl texting and walking got kissed by the bumper of a 4Runner crossing the street in front of me. She fell to the ground and laughed because she was surprised she didn't break her phone.

"Well, I'll tell you what happened, but it goes without saying that I would prefer to keep a lid on it. I don't need any more drama right now." I was fragile. I didn't even want to think about what people were saying about me but at the same time it was all I could think about.

"Of course, I got you. I just wanted to hear it from the horse's mouth. After mom and dad and Fritz's theories, I'm just tired and want to hear this from you."

Fritz is my step dad, and possibly a candidate for sainthood. He and my mom had known one another forever because they worked at the Cleveland Clinic together. When my parents divorced, Fritz asked my mom out and the rest is history. He grew up in Bay City, MI in a house the size of a closet. He was the son of a high school physics teacher and a mother who was old-school, the kind of woman who would tell him to stay away from girls because they're all hussies. He is now one of the world's leading surgeons specializing in erectile dysfunction. He has a few penile prosthetics patented. He also more than likely has some form of Asperger's syndrome, which makes things even more interesting. He covers up a lot of his social awkwardness by telling jokes, usually penis jokes or other sexually related things. Once, on Christmas Eve, we went to mass and he told our pastor this joke:

"Father Snow (yes, his name is Snow), ask me what I got for Christmas...I got a sweater, but what I really wanted was a screamer or a moaner."

To my pleasure, I have so many more stories similar to this. I'll never forget the look on that priest's face.

I took a breath and began to fill Megan in on how I'd found myself in my current state. I told her that Erin and I had left Portland right on time. Erin got pulled over in Hood River which is only an hour into the trip. That wouldn't have been notable except that I had an eight ball of coke in my ski boot so obviously, I was terrified. Thankfully the cop let us go, mostly because Erin melted him within two seconds of looking at her. So that was a close call. I drove the rest of the way. Pat and Tim had already gotten to Bacon's house in Missoula and were waiting for us. The drive wasn't too bad at all until the end because it was dark and snowing. I was tired and just wanted to see those guys and start drinking.

Megan already knew that Erin was a hostess at the restaurant where I worked. She's twenty-three, an only child, and is a Portland native. She was raised solely by her mother. Her mom worked in government relations or something like that and spent some time in the Philippines in the 90's, had a fling with a dude there, and Erin is the product of that fling. She quite literally looks like an Asian version of Rihanna. She's stunning. She makes most of her money modeling, along with various other hobbies including, but not limited to, industrial leather working, tuning motorcycles and herding cattle. Much of her life is her image. She puts more thought into what/who she's

124

going to be for the day than I put into a month of who I'm not going to be, but we're both insecure in our own ways.

For as attractive as she is, she is kind of tragic in my eyes. Most of her friends are males, and they're usually twice her age, and often rough looking. Her attractiveness is debilitating, in a way. She's too young and not aware enough to be living in the body she resides in. Usually when I meet a girl and she doesn't have any "girl friends" it's a red flag that they're unpredictably predictable. When she started working with me, I took one look at her and knew she would be trouble for me if I pursued her. I also felt she was way out of my league. I barely talked to her, and even made a point not to until Christmas rolled around and a friend bailed on me for the Johnny Mathis Christmas concert at the Schnitz. I haphazardly talked about it at the bar and she was sitting there and perked up, showing interest, so I invited her, and she came.

We hit it off, and started spending a lot of time together. On Valentine's Day, she and my best friend Jeff and I went to the strip club. Jeff and I got drunk and were paying the strippers to slap us. It was classy. I really liked Erin, against my better judgment. Everyone at work told me it was a bad idea. I never thought I could land a girl this attractive and was feeling great about the fact that she liked me. She really did like me.

I told Megan that when we arrived at Bacon's house, Pat and Tim had gone to the store and cooked a massive dinner. They had brought out all of Bacon's nice dinnerware and lit candles and whatnot. They made a full cheese plate with this peppered sausage that I love. Tim made pistachio encrusted halibut steaks with cauliflower rice and Pat made prosciutto wrapped asparagus. It was such a nice treat to walk into a warm house and see those guys with an amazing meal waiting. Naturally, Erin hit it off with them immediately and was already flirting. After dinner, I told them I brought dessert and busted out the coke. It was strong, and on par with the Cleveland cocaine we were used to. I smashed the whole thing out and we started going to town on it while crushing gin and grapefruit juice. We should have started off a little smaller, but whenever I get together with those guys, we have little to no self-control.

"Yeah, you guys are ridiculous. Was Erin doing any coke?" Megan wanted to know the details.

They really didn't matter, but I guess Megan wanted to implicate Erin in her mind because she wanted to hate her without knowing her.

"Kind of, she was playing with it a bunch and kind of pretending like she knew what she was doing but whatever..."

"Ha, so she's kind of a poser when it comes to that stuff?"

"More or less, I dunno, she just thought we wouldn't have thought she was cool if she didn't do it or something, who knows…"

I told Megan that eventually another friend and his girlfriend came over too, which was great because I hadn't seen him since Christmas. We all went downtown to the bar Charley B's, the main dive bar in Missoula. At the bar, Erin was all fucked up and out of her element. She was trying to keep up with us and she definitely couldn't. She was sloppy and all over the place, although compared to the general population of locals, she probably only stood out based on her beauty. I didn't really give a shit because I knew she was coming home with *me* and acting jealous is a great way to look like a douche bag. I went outside to smoke with Pat and he told me he thought Erin was trouble. His advice: "That's the kind of girl you bang as long as you can and when it's done you just pat yourself on the back and move on."

We kept railing coke in the bathroom and drinking with too much tenacity. We finally made it back to the house and kept drinking. Erin went and passed out on the futon and I kind of forgot about her. We raged a little longer and when I realized it was five in the morning I went upstairs to go to bed. Within a few minutes, I realized I needed water so I went back downstairs. As I passed the futon I saw Erin's head pop up. I cautiously said, "Hey, uhhh how ya doin?"

In the early morning haze, her face looked guilty—deer in headlights, caught with one's pants down, etc. Whatever image paints it best. To me, she looked like she was fucking my best friends and I immediately began to lose it. I asked her who else was on the futon. She said, "Pat and Tim."

"Fuckin Patrick," Megan said. She knew that Pat had a reputation for fucking friends' girlfriends. It's a difficult thing to explain, but that should explain it. Tim wasn't very different. Tim had actually slept with my sister once.

"Yeah," I said. I knew that Megan had already made her mind up about the situation. I knew she already had the ending written, which is why the real ending is the worst part of this whole ordeal, and it doesn't come remotely close to being a true ending, but arguably the beginning of something much more sordid.

The truth is, Erin didn't fuck Pat. Sure, it looked really bad—all of the ingredients were there. But Pat had drunkenly passed out on the futon not realizing that Erin was already sleeping there, and Tim crashed in after him. I walked in right at the moment they hit the futon and she popped up looking like I had caught them all. Erin ran up to me, grabbed my arms and frantically asked me what was wrong. I wanted to kill her. "Let's go to bed love. Let's go upstairs and go to bed. Nothing was going on, he just passed out and woke me up."

I didn't even bother to try and talk to the guys, but I couldn't have. They were passed out, and didn't do anything wrong. We were all so fucked up. I found out later that Tim wound up puking all over the place and Pat didn't even remember half the night.

Erin kept trying to get me to talk but I peeled her arms off mine and walked into the laundry room where I had a giant purple bucket with all of my clothes. I picked it up, walked out the front door, got in my car, and left. I left Erin in Missoula and drove blacked out drunk and high on cocaine for three hours to Whitefish. She wound up having to catch a ride to Bozeman and fly back to Portland on her own dime, alone.

Apparently after I left, she woke Pat up and explained that I hopped in my car and left and he called everyone that we knew in Missoula. He called our friend, who we were with earlier, he called my ex-girlfriend, who now lived in Missoula. Then he called the police and my parents in Cleveland. He called my sister. Before too long a missing persons alert went out and the entire state of Montana was looking for me. I had turned my phone off so no one could find me and by the skin of my teeth, had made it to Whitefish. Also, by some grace of God, Dagmara answered her phone at eight in the morning and let me into her house. She saved my life. It was one of the most disgraceful events of my life, and if I wasn't so insecure and wasn't a raging alcoholic and cocaine addict, not all, but most of this could have been

129

avoided. I left a girl who did nothing wrong in Montana. I told her mom I'd keep her safe and take care of her. I didn't. I almost killed myself over something I fabricated in my head due to extreme insecurity. That was almost a year ago, and I still see Erin at work every day.

Colombia

Dagmara and I had a lot of heart-to-hearts in Montana before I would return to Portland to atone for my colossal mishap with Erin.

"What truly makes you happy, Murray?" she asked one night.

"I guess, traveling—traveling and volunteering. I loved all of the time I spent in Honduras working at orphanages and all that."

"Well, how about this: I have a good friend, Marie, and she's going to be traveling through South America this summer. You should join her. I know she's looking for someone to accompany her. You'd love her…"

I thought about this for a second. People are always telling me to meet their friends, you know, "Hey I have a friend you'd really love, and you have a lot in common…etc." The reality is that I never follow through with any of these recommendations because I am so insecure and don't want to disappoint anyone that has set me up. In this case though, I was so embarrassed and depressed about my latest fuck-up that I didn't really care.

Dagmara contacted Marie and told her I was interested in possibly joining her. She put Marie and I in touch, and almost immediately upon returning to

Portland I began chatting with her regularly. She was also from Cleveland but the only mutual friend we had was Dagmara, who had mentioned her a few times over the years. I'd seen pictures of her too, and she was exactly my type; petite, brunette, sexy, hippie.

Marie and I would chat for around an hour at a time and I began to learn a lot about her. I told her about me, probably too much. I always tell people way too many details about myself immediately, over half of which are usually extremely embellished. I wanted Marie to love me even before I met her. I thought I loved her already.

We talked about our families, about Yoga. We'd share our favorite Dead shows. She hated Phish which was always a funny topic of conversation because I love them. We talked about our past relationships and all that. I really felt that I knew her.

Marie emailed me a rough itinerary of her travel plans and left it open to me when and where I'd join her. I decided to meet her in Bogota, Colombia on June 29th. I'd spend a few weeks traveling with her through Colombia and Ecuador volunteering with two different agencies. At the time we were planning this, I was taking a full load of grad school credits working on my master's thesis. I remember sitting in the grad lab and taking care of my travel insurance, signing up and applying for the different volunteer programs.

When my departure date got closer, I told my boss that I was going to leave for a month. I told her that I was going to Colombia to volunteer. Before I hatched this new Fall-In-Love Plan, I was planning on following Phish for the summer, which would have meant hitting about nine shows up and down the west coast with my friends, eating drugs, spending all my money on booze, blacking out and probably not remembering half of it. I presented this traveling opportunity as a more mature alternative.

My boss was totally fine with it, she was even excited for me. I didn't tell her that I was going to be meeting a girl there that I was already, in my mind, in love with. The difference between love and obsession wasn't clear to me. I didn't tell my boss, or anyone for that matter that I'd be meeting Marie because to them, I would have been setting up the exact scenario that played out in Montana with Erin. Knowing that the people who love me would worry about me defaulting to my classic patterns, to the extent that I actually hid all the facts from them, should have been a sign, but of course, old habits die hard.

Instead of listening to my gut, I created a narrative in my head before I left for Colombia. It sounded something like this:

I go to Colombia out of a desire to do some good and help people in an impoverished country in lieu of wasting my time at Phish. I happen to be doing this good work alongside a beautiful girl. I get to show this girl that I am a sensitive, caring individual who likes to spend his time volunteering, practicing yoga, listening to great music, and writing poetry. She falls in love with me, and then I return to the states with a girlfriend, maybe even a wife...a hot hippie-chick who's into all the same things I am. We have beautiful kids and go to live shows together hand in hand and buy a cute little house. Maybe we even adopt a kid from Colombia!

At the same time I was planning this trip with my future wife, I was seeing another girl named Serena. Serena was totally cute, into cooking, rock climbing, yoga...but in hindsight, I think I really liked Serena because our mutual friend said I would. It's as though I didn't want to disappoint anyone by failing to live up to their assumptions of me.

Serena and I had been set up at the Mercado one night by the mutual friend and talked over Sangria and tacos. This led to an invitation to hang at her place to cook vegan food and watch one of my favorite movies, *Fried Green Tomatoes*. This inevitably led to making out ferociously until her roommate walked in on us. I did love making out with Serena.

I told her I was leaving for South America soon, and at the time, she was supposed to be moving to Hawaii to work on an organic farm for free room and board. Since we were both already in the process of planning the next phases of our lives, we decided to simply "enjoy one another's company" until we parted ways. Of course, that didn't happen.

It wasn't long before we were basically dating. We spent most nights cooking, fucking, hiking in the gorge, drinking more sangria at the Mercado. We were a couple. I knew before long that she was attached to me, or at least the idea of me that I presented to her.

I kept who I was going to travel to Colombia with vague. I told her that I was going with a platonic friend-of-a-friend that was also interested in volunteering. There was no way I was going to jeopardize the convenience of getting laid by a hot rock climber.

I do this thing where I start to make it obvious that I am eternally self-destructing to women I am sleeping with that I know will go nowhere. It's the only time I actually *try* to show people the real me; when I don't want them anymore but I still need them to love me. I started doing this with Serena. I started drinking hard in front of her with my friends. I'd show up to dates high as fuck on coke. I'd smoke cigarettes in front of her even though I knew she hated it. I wanted her to hate me before I left for Colombia so it would be easy for me to walk away. It didn't work. We spent the rest of June still dating. I met all of her friends and I made them love me. I manipulated, lied, and did everything I could to keep her attached while also trying to make her walk away.

One of the last times we hung out was when the Cavs played the Golden State Warriors in the National Championship. We went to her friend's house and watched it on their porch. I remember her sitting on my lap. She was beautiful, stunning really. We were still being cute, couple-y, even though I knew in two days I'd be on to my next victim. After the Cavs won, we went and bought a bottle of champagne and drank it at my house. She surprised me with a bunch of presents for my trip: boxes of Luna Bars with little labels that read "When the food sucks and you're starving for some sustenance," hand sanitizer that read, "Wash your hands! Don't get sick, a small hand-sewn stuffed penguin. There was also a handmade card with a picture of a dinosaur eating a little human that had a bubble that read "I could just eat you up!" The human was supposed to be me, I think.

These were all things to remind me of her; to make me realize that she actually loved me and couldn't wait for me to return because at this point, she had bagged the idea of going to Hawaii. We had sex and then she watched me pack all the gifts into my bag. I also packed a bunch of condoms when she wasn't looking.

Once I finished packing, I sat Serena down and told her not to wait around for me. I told her that if someone else came along in my absence that she should act on it. She read between the lines: "I'm not in love with you—don't get your hopes up."

I knew a day later I'd be in the arms of Marie, the Marie of my bullshit narrative and dreams or whatever you want to call it—let's call it delusion. Serena left my house sobbing. I had stomped on her heart with one foot, and the other was already out the door ready to take me to Marie.

Later, I'd tell her everything that happened, apologize, and she'd forgive me. Later, Serena would find a guy that loved her and he'd propose. Later, I'd tell her that she deserved much more than what I had pretended to offer. Later, I'd realize how poorly I treated her and she'd read excerpts from this book on Instagram and write me an encouraging comment about how she's happy that I'm still around, and that she was proud of me.

The first night in Colombia, Marie and I arrived at the volunteer house via cab after she waited for me at the airport. We set down our stuff, and me, not knowing any other way to break the ice, asked Marie if she wanted to go wander around and grab a drink. I'd find out immediately that she wasn't a drinker. Her dad was a drinker and a smoker and it bothered her. We went to Simon Bolivar park and sat on a swing set. I drank a bottle of wine almost completely to myself and we ate a bit of chocolate.

In the next hour or so, Marie would tell me more about her past relationships, especially the most recent one that had sparked her interest in traveling

137

alone for the summer. She'd also make it clear that she wasn't looking for anything more from me than a fellow traveling partner and someone to have casual sex with. I remember feeling utter despair, which was pathetic because she had just told me she wanted to fuck around and travel, no strings attached. Why couldn't I be okay with this? Instead, I felt hurt and like I had already blown something. I became hell-bent on changing her mind, I was going to make her love me, after all, I had just left a perfectly "normal relationship" for her- repetitive, self-torturous behavior is a drug to me.

I woke up the next morning hating myself as I thought about everything that Marie had said. I remember writing, "you fucking fool, you did it again" in the small notebook I'd brought with me. Sadly, that would be all I'd write in that little notebook the whole trip. I did, however, decide that I was going to be the most positive, hilarious person she'd ever met; maybe then she'd change her mind, maybe then she'd love me.

The day after we arrived we had two days off from work. We traveled to Villa De Leyva, a small town about an hour away from Bogota. We rented a room in a small hostel off the town square. We bummed around all day and ate. I drank. We met a friend of mine from Portland that was also in Colombia. He had begun dating a lovely Colombian girl named Anna. We'd wind up hanging with them quite a bit which was perfect for me because I got to play "couples."

Our first night in the hostel, our room had two single beds. Going to bed separately, I remember laying there wondering how and when I was going to ask to climb into bed with her. It felt like eternity, but eventually I asked. She laughed a little and said, "Yeah get over here." We spooned until we fell asleep and when we woke up we had sex for the first time. It was short and to the point. I remember once I was inside of her she sighed and said, "Ugh, it's been like, over a month. I needed this!" as if I was taking her out for a coffee. I couldn't concentrate because I was hungover and all I could think was "You've gotta make this girl cum man. You've gotta do the best job ever so she wants more and falls in love with you..." Another part of me was saying, "This girl really just wants to fuck Murray, don't get attached..." It's funny how trying to do better at this only made me more mediocre and pathetic in the end.

For the most part, the next few weeks went well. I kept my shit together and focused on having fun while trying not to think of the ending.

I loved hanging out with my Portland friend and Anna's family, especially the day we tagged along to a Land Rover gathering/convention with over one-thousand other die-hard Land Rover owners. The day ended with the most delicious arepas and yogurt I'll ever have.

I loved going to the park every day after volunteering, doing a small amount of Yoga, having sex in my hammock, and napping.

I loved cooking for Marie any chance I had. We quickly became bored of the food at the volunteer house so I'd go to the market for supplies and cook her fancy dinners, you know, to show her what a life with me could look like.

I loved becoming close and traveling with an Australian couple, Ben and Emma, who are still dear friends of mine.

I loved working at the orphanage with Marie-watching the kids and taking them to their music lesson, feeding them in the morning and before we laid them down for their nap. She was so good with the kids, I'd think to myself, *she'd be the best mother.*

I loved traveling on our days off, staying at cool Airbnb's or hotels and eating at the best restaurants I could find. Everything was so cheap. Sometimes at restaurants and on airlines we'd tell staff we were on our honeymoon so they'd give us upgrades or free drinks.

I loved going paragliding in Medellin toward the end of the trip. We also floated down a river that met the ocean in Palomino. We rented horses for a sunset trail ride up the mountain that finished with us galloping into the sunset. I was high on cocaine and it was probably one of my favorite parts of the trip. I knew that once we returned to Cleveland, she'd forget about me, so that night I tried to enjoy and appreciate everything about her. Seeing her ride that horse with the orange creamsicle glow of the sunset will be something I'll never forget or regret. I cried like a little baby the whole ride.

There were plenty of beautiful moments and stretches of days where I kept it together, but eventually, like always, I fell apart. One week of our trip was spent volunteering with All Hands in Canoa, Ecuador. This is when the vibe of the trip really began to change. Canoa had been devastated by a series of earthquakes that reduced the entire coastline to rubble. Up until that point it had been somewhat of a secret destination for surfers. Our job was to clean up the aftermath and build new homes from bamboo using the most primitive tools and intense manual labor.

Most of the other volunteers had been there much longer and were there immediately following the quakes to dig bodies out of the fallen buildings. These people were what I'd call the "not fucking around" types who gave up a normal life and chased natural disasters and contributed to making the world a slightly less-shitty place on the regular.

I felt insecure around these people from the get-go. While Marie continued to flit around, happily lending help and socializing, I began to hit a wall.

Our schedule was grueling, we woke up at 5:30am every day to (maybe) a cold shower and were allotted one banana, two eggs, and a croissant for breakfast. After, we'd move on to our respective projects which were assigned every night at a mandatory debriefing where we'd talk about each day's struggles and accomplishments.

Marie and I didn't work together once, and after the day was over we'd both be so exhausted that we'd crawl into a tiny little tent we bought at a mall and try to sleep. Half the time I couldn't fall asleep because I was being eaten by mosquitos. This was during the Zika outbreak and three other volunteers had to leave because they had become infected.

I started paying for a room in a hostel down the road so we'd have a bed and a shower, and also with the intention of getting laid.

My attitude began to plummet every day because my perfect little vacation I had dreamt up was becoming a nightmare. The days were long and hotter than hell. Most of the other volunteers either. didn't like me or I couldn't stand them. In my mind, they were all pretentious, sanctimonious assholes who were sick of what I thought then was "real life." Mostly, they were just decent people who wanted to help humanity and I was angry and jealous that Marie had hit it off with all of them. I was also drinking my ass off every night. I'd cut coconuts from the trees, crack them open, and pour whatever booze I could find inside of them and chug it until I ran out, then I'd buy beers.

The night that I finally snapped Marie and I got in a huge fight. Or rather, I drunkenly screamed at her. At that point I knew when the trip ended, nothing would come of the two of us. I had looked in her phone while she was in the shower and read a conversation she'd been having with a friend from home. It was the classic mistake of being an insecure nosy little baby and reading a "girlfriend's" text messages. What a fool. I tried calling Marie out for leading me on and only telling me she loved me because she didn't want me to flip out. She told me I was being ridiculous and to go to bed, and that she wasn't going to argue with a drunk. I threatened to leave her there, which in hindsight, she would have been fine with. I huffed and puffed and wandered around on the beach crying and stomping around because I knew if I hadn't blown it yet, I surely had now. Eventually I climbed into bed and passed out.

I woke up the next morning and apologized profusely as she held my hand with a kind of pity. It was as though she actually felt bad for me and how much of an asshole I had been. We left that volunteer site a day early. She was so finished with me and was such a good sport by not leaving me on a street corner weeks earlier. I took her kind gesture as a reason to concoct a new ending to our month-long tryst: since we were both flying back to Cleveland for a time, we'd hang out there and fuck a few more times and meet each other's friends/family, show everyone our pictures and tell our stories. As I left the Bogota airport, I told her I loved her and not to make me wait too long before I would see her again.

When I arrived in Cleveland, I was in great spirits. I truly felt on top of the world; I think they call this "delusions of grandeur."

When Marie didn't respond to any of my messages for three days, I decided it was a good time to completely self-destruct. I got so drunk at the Lakeside Yacht Club after day drinking and snorting coke on my buddy's boat that I had what in hindsight was a drug-fueled panic attack. I almost checked myself into the psych ward that night. It had only been three days since I got back and I was due at my best friend's shotgun wedding a few days later. It was not the best time to lose my shit. I was also about to join my family in South Carolina for a vacation. Yes, another vacation after a month in South America; I have a rough life.

When I woke up one morning I had a missed call from Marie, I called her back immediately. Apparently, I had called bawling the night before telling her I missed her in some shitty voicemail. Classic.

I begged her to hang out with me. She reluctantly obliged. She drove across Cleveland to my mom's house and met her briefly. I showed her around my childhood home and tried to be cute and affectionate toward her though it was clear she wasn't interested. I tried to keep it together. I took her to a little village down the street and to the bar I used to manage. Why I thought it would be a good idea to take her to a bar is beyond me. We went for ice cream after. I thought she'd want to hang out all night and maybe sleep over, but she had made plans. She left. I started drinking.

It wasn't long until I was sending somber passive/aggressive texts to her. Of course, she had the maturity not to respond. Somehow, we hung out twice more before I left for my family vacation. First, we went bowling, she was an hour late, then I took her to my favorite restaurant and we ate lobster bisque and parted ways.

The last time I saw Marie we had planned to meet at a movie theater near her house to see *The Secret Life of Pets*. I went an hour early and hit a happy hour nearby at Longhorn Steakhouse. I was trying not to smell like booze, so I ordered espresso martinis. I think I had five in an hour.

She was late for the movie. I was sitting outside waiting since we agreed to see the next showing. Something I've never really mastered is the art of covering up the fact that I am shitfaced, it's unbelievably awkward.

I had also gone out of my way to procure backstage VIP passes to a Grateful Dead gathering for her and her friend. They were valued at $600 a ticket but a friend had given them to me for free. Who knows what my intention was behind this, I suppose some pathetic final attempt at making her feel guilty enough to hang out with me.

We walked into the movie and they had those new seats that recline, I tried holding her hand and she shrugged it away. Then she said, "You're drunk, don't cause a scene." I threw the envelope with the VIP passes at her and walked out of the theater.

I was fuming angry, heartbroken, and embarrassed. She texted me from inside the theater, "Are you coming back!? What was that all about? Why are you drunk!?"

I begged her to come out and talk to me, she made me promise not to scream at her or cause a scene, which of course, I did. We agreed to go to a park she liked nearby and talk for our final time.

I told her she had led me on. I tried pleading and begging for sympathy. I reminded her of times she showed me love to make her feel bad for leaving me this way, even though in order for someone to leave someone else, they need to be together in the first place. She wouldn't budge. I hugged her for a really long time and drove back to the east side of Cleveland, went to a bar, and blacked out...I would never see Marie again.

She sent me two messages days later; one with pictures of new Grateful Dead Chacos she had bought, another asking how the wedding had gone, and how my vacation in South Carolina was going. I knew she didn't really care. Why should she have?

When I finally returned to Portland, I wrote her a long message asking her to leave me alone and once again, tried evoking sympathy by letting my suffering be known.

She responded with, "If you really don't want to hear from me anymore, then I'll leave you alone. I hope your days get brighter! Take care."

Depression

When I returned from Colombia, I had what I guess most people would refer to as a complete nervous breakdown. My brain became a hellish sinkhole that I couldn't pull myself out of. I wanted to die. I couldn't think straight. I couldn't sleep. I didn't want to see friends. I was drinking hard. After three or four days of self-medicating, in a stroke of genius, I decided that maybe drinking was a bad idea. I went to an old shrink of mine at the Cleveland Clinic and told them everything. I told them that I was exhausted, that I wanted to die, that I hated myself and that I couldn't go on.

They asked, "if we had a magic wand right now that would make this all better, what would you ask me to do?"

I had no answer. I wanted to fall asleep and not wake up. I didn't want to go back to Portland because I hated it there, I didn't want to stay in Cleveland because I hated it there too. At that time, if someone offered me a one-way ticket to a private island with all the things I love, I would have declined the offer.

Once I mentioned all of this to the shrink, they asked if I wanted to be admitted to the psychiatric unit for a stay. This is how I imagined this would have looked: Two men would have been called into the office. They would escort me down a hallway to a room where I'd take off all of my clothes and change into some smock or gown made of fabric that rips with too much tension in case I tried to hang myself with it. Then I'd be "processed" (asked a bunch of leading questions), given some sort of sedative and locked in a room with a camera glaring at me. I didn't want this.

They asked if I had made a plan. Like, a plan to kill myself. Shit, I'd made hundreds. If you're drinking from a cup made from recycled paper right now, your lips are likely grazing the shredded pieces of one of my many attempts at a suicide note. I had, of course, mostly considered the most painless and clean ways to die:

- Buy some heroin and overdose
- Take a heap of pills
- Do the ol' car in the garage thing

I thought about drowning myself, but Lake Erie is disgusting and I hate being dirty so that would have had to happen back in Oregon in the Pacific, you know, if I made it back.

I answered "no" to the plan question. I knew I had to be very careful about letting them know how truly depressed I was. I didn't want to be locked up against my will.

The next thing on the docket was being put on Lithium. "What the fuck?" I thought, "That's what crazy people take!"

They claimed the Lithium would curb my suicidal ideations, and in that moment a prescription sounded preferable to a padded cell. They wrote me a script and told me to call for a check-in before I returned to Oregon. However, upon leaving the office, I threw the paper in the trash. I told myself, "You can totally do this without taking crazy people pills…"

I'd also mentioned that I wanted to stop drinking. They asked if I'd ever heard of a pill called Antabuse. I knew that using this drug was an archaic method in quenching an alcoholic's urge to drink. Basically, you take this pill every morning and if you drink any alcohol at all, you become violently ill and projectile vomit. There weren't any alarming side effects (other than the obvious vomiting) so I decided to take it. Let's be real, I'm always down for some self-punishment and I loathe getting sick, so the combination of these outcomes would surely keep me from boozing. I filled that script, as Antabuse didn't fall under the umbrella of "crazy people pills" I was attempting to avoid.

I didn't actually start taking the Antabuse until after the wedding and family vacation. The fact that I went two days without drinking leading up to my best friend's wedding was actually quite astonishing, what with all my childhood friends present and ready to rage.

I kept it together for the entire day of the wedding. In fact, I woke up early and went swimming in a

150

nearby lake with the groom. Afterwards, we went to his parent's house and prepared everything for the event. We hung Edison light bulbs, arranged tables and chairs, groomed the yard, set up fire pits, garbage cans, etc. I actually enjoyed doing these tasks—they served as a distraction from my desperate and crazy thoughts.

As a reward for our efforts—and because we are privileged white males who certainly don't have any business being depressed—we took a steam bath at the Cleveland Racquet Club before getting dressed in our suits and heading to Gesu, the very grade school parish from which we graduated.

Spending time with Bucky that day was extremely important to me. It was his big day, and my depression and bullshit simply had to be put aside for his sake and everyone else's. I suppose it leads me to believe that feelings are more within our control than we assume.

The wedding was beautiful, and I went *almost* the entire evening without having a single cocktail. Things started winding down around midnight and most of the adults had left. I drove my sisters and my parents back to their house, which was right down the road. When I got home, I drank a half bottle of single malt scotch as quickly as I could and went back to the party. As I said, *almost.*

151

We left for our family vacation one day later. I continued to busy myself by heading to the Apple store just before leaving, to pick out a new computer so that I'd have something to write with while there. My thesis would be due the coming spring and I needed to start working on it, in case I didn't kill myself.

The vacation was bittersweet. Everyone in my family knew I was fucked up in the head and essentially forced me go along because they didn't feel comfortable allowing me to return to Portland without supervision.

I drank a good amount during the vacation, and continued my high-functioning ways; I cooked a lot, rode a bike around, went for beach walks at sunset with my sisters and swam in the pool. I was taking a lot of Ativan to keep me from completely freaking out. I had intimate talks with my mom. We always celebrate my baby sister's birthday while we're on vacation and I made her bacon wrapped scallops with a sweet corn succotash. We baked a cake and played some board games. It shouldn't have been about me, but I was having a hard time holding it together. Even through the foggy lenses of my depressed state, I could see my family clearly tiptoeing around me.

Much to my delight, I was upgraded to first class on my return flight to Portland. It was a five-hour direct flight from CLE to PDX, and first class meant free booze. I drank two glasses of champagne before the plane took off and drank a bottle and a half of shitty red wine during the flight. Eventually, I passed out.

I woke up in Portland unable to see straight and with a head-full of chaos: Classes were about to resume and I dreaded returning to a windowless classroom with peers that flat-out didn't like me. I didn't want to write. I didn't want to listen or talk or think. I didn't want to do anything. The only activity I could muster was meeting up with people to drink.

Luckily, my restaurant job, which I truly loved, was still available and my boss asked if I wanted to return to work. The restaurant had become my home and a safe place, work had become family. My co-workers had witnessed my ups and downs, my messy entanglements with women, my insanity, and my drinking and for whatever reason, they still accepted me. When I was spinning out, my boss had a way of reeling me in and reminding me of how good I actually had it. She would say, "Hey Murray, there are a lot of people out there who have it way worse than you do..." Not groundbreaking information, but for some reason, coming from *her*, it meant something. My depression became selfish and sadness was my luxury. I couldn't be upset around her. I couldn't be upset at work. It was the only constant that I had in Portland. Even in this moment, I know I'll never find another place like it. I miss it.

Even though I had my job back, a group of friends that loved me, and a stable place to live—all the makings of a happy human—I was stuck in a mental loop of suffering I couldn't shake. I still constantly wanted to die. I called my shrink in Cleveland ("sorry I forgot to check-in before I left!") and they called in a new prescription for Lithium to the local Safeway Pharmacy. I filled it hours later and reluctantly swallowed the first pill, along with the Antabuse.

The next morning, I wrote this journal entry in the Stickies app on my computer:

Tuesday September 13th, 2016

Last night I walked through Safeway on Powell Boulevard to pick up my first prescription for Lithium. I haven't been on anything like this since I was sent away to boarding school when I was seventeen. Wait, that's not entirely true, I hit a spot of depression while living in Madison, WI—it had to be the winter of 2008. I tried taking Seroquel and a bunch of other meds they threw at me. That was a bad idea.

I walked through the soda aisle feeling ashamed, defeated, and completely helpless. A week or so ago my psychiatrist gave me a prescription for Lithium— I tore it up and threw it in the trash as I left the building without any intention of taking it. I kept telling myself that it wasn't necessary and that I could do this all on my own. This just isn't the case.

After receiving a text from Marie asking if I was back in Portland, I lost it. I responded with a text I had written almost a week prior, asking her never to speak to me again.

When I woke up and swallowed the first pill this morning, I felt disgusting. I kept thinking of the litany of side effects:

- *drowsiness*
- *tremors in your hands*
- *dry mouth, increased thirst or urination*
- *nausea, vomiting, loss of appetite, stomach pain*
- *changes in your skin or hair*
- *cold feeling or discoloration in your fingers or toes*
- *feeling uneasy*
- *impotence, loss of interest in sex.*

What the fuck right? Jesus. For countless years psychiatrists have been trying to diagnose me with bipolar disorder. After watching a slideshow that, very simply, breaks down the symptoms of bipolar disorder, I am acknowledging that I, without any shred of doubt, am bipolar. I can't stand the thought of calling myself someone with this disorder. I feel it's a cop-out, an excuse to walk around and try to

155

rationalize all of my erratic thoughts and behavior for the last, well, twenty-nine years. I turn thirty in two weeks.

I drove to my friend's house to trim weed for $25 an hour to begin the long slow process of making back all the money which will have gone to my life's most expensive mistake: Colombia. I have also been taking Antabuse. I haven't had a drink yet, not a sip. I ebb and flow between feeling good about this and just wanting a fucking drink. I guess I feel better that I'm not giving half of my next day to the night prior and racking up $50 bar tabs. Maybe I should feel good about the fact that it didn't take me killing someone with my car from the endless amounts of times I've woken up and realized that I drove home blacked out.

I've been thinking about killing myself something like every five minutes. I was thinking about doing it on my thirtieth birthday. I thought about going in a week early and buying a pistol from Mark, the same guy who sold me my surfboard. He also sells guns: both things that can kill people, maybe. I was thinking I'd go to Indian Beach and surf for as long as possible and then take as much Ativan as I could stomach, then I'd shoot myself in the heart, facing the ocean. The fact that I'd be wearing a wetsuit would keep it from being too messy. I keep telling myself to at least write an apology to the person

or people who'd find me, but then I'd have to write
everyone an apology. The thing is, I know that most
people wouldn't be surprised, and maybe they'd never
forgive me, or it might ruin their lives, but they
would probably understand.

    My mom called me right as I got to work. I
showed up early after attending a seven-a.m. yoga
class. I haven't been able to sleep. Whether my eyes
are open or closed I can't stop thinking and feeling
and hating everything. Marie flashes into my mind
everywhere and at all moments. I keep wondering
how long it will take, if ever, for me to reach a place
where I think about her and feel nothing. At this rate,
never.

    My mom asked how I was and I told her I had
talked to the same psychiatrist who aided in sending
me to boarding school, and I told him I was still mis-
erable and wanted to die, and that I agreed to start
the Lithium. She reacted by telling me she was con-
cerned that it wasn't necessary, and she shared her
own experiences of anxiety that she had never shared
with me before and then she started crying telling
me that I couldn't kill myself. The pain in her voice
only hurt me more. I told her that she needed to stop.
She kept saying, "After all the bullshit you and I have
endured and been through sweetie?" We had endured
quite a bit. This was true.

What's funny is I didn't read this dramatically depressing and spastic journal entry until a few weeks ago when I was lying in bed in Bali looking for an excuse not to write this book. I was combing through old documents and files, tripping down memory lane, and I had completely forgotten that I'd written this. I read it, and actually started laughing. I brought it out to Hanna and read it to her. She asked how I felt about my bipolar diagnosis now. Then she reminded me that my thirtieth birthday had come and gone and I was still around; she asked me how I felt about that.

I'm definitely not bipolar, not a chance. Why I felt that I was? Because I was desperately seeking an answer or a convenient way to help me understand me. If you have a medical degree, you are a doctor. If you write a book, you are an author. If you have symptoms of bipolar disorder, you are bipolar. Great, at least I could blame something seemingly tangible—a disease. As much as I say that I felt defeated and against being labeled as someone with this disorder, there was a subtle amount of comfort in giving in to whatever labels were put on me by my doctors.

The months between Labor Day weekend and Thanksgiving were miserable. I wasn't drinking, I was taking a full load of credits preparing for my thesis defense, and working as a lead bartender five nights a week. Since cocaine in Portland is easier to get than an Uber, I began buying and snorting it regularly with the money I would have otherwise been spending on booze. My birthday was coming up and I was in constant contact with my mom and my team of shrinks back in Cleveland checking in with them almost every day. My mom flew my best friend Bucky out to visit me from Cleveland for the weekend, Jeff drove up from Santa Rosa and Tim drove down from Seattle. Having those three with me for my birthday was huge. I didn't drink the entire time they were there, but I did do a lot of nitrous oxide. This certainly wasn't the greatest idea, but I had such a hard time staying sober around friends, and clearly had no clue how to be "fun" without substances, so I justified getting high as the lesser of two evils.

I was still showing up to work and school and doing the best I could. I was attending yoga every day at Yoga Union (another place where I found a sense of home, support and kinship) and soon enough the snow would fall and I could focus the rest of my efforts on skiing at Mt. Hood. This is when I received another blow—my right shoulder began to hurt quite a bit and I feared the worst. I had already sustained a shoulder injury from Yoga in June of 2012. I knew in my heart that I had injured my other shoulder from doing yoga, as well. I scheduled an MRI a week later. The results showed that I had done the exact same thing to my right shoulder as I had my left. When I had an appointment with the orthopedic surgeon and she told me I needed surgery, I responded with this:

Look, I'm depressed and suicidal most days.

Yoga is the only positive, healthy thing I am doing for myself.

It's going to snow soon and I'm not going to give up skiing, either.

I won't be able to drive my car because it's a manual transmission and I need my right hand.

I bartend for a living and need my hands and arms 24/7 to do this to pay for grad school.

There's no fucking way I'm having another shoulder surgery.

I walked out of the office with a DVD file of my MRI.

When I told the yoga studio that I was injured, they disproved my World-Is-Out-To-Get-Me Theory and gave me my $1,200 back and sent a "get well" card to my house along with a note inviting me to use their sauna for free whenever I wanted. That meant a great deal to me.

I continued working and going to school, taking Antabuse, Lithium, and didn't drink even though I was doing more coke than ever. Every few weeks I'd drive to OHSU and have my blood drawn (which I hate) so they could monitor my Lithium levels. I was lonelier than I'd ever been in my life. In the beginning, I tried going out with friends to shows and bars and resuming my normal life in Portland, but I quickly began to realize that my anxiety was out of control when in public. I would try to socialize and have normal conversations with my friends, but they were all getting hammered and trying to talk to them felt pointless. Three things that I noticed about not drinking and telling people I didn't drink was:

1) People say, "I'm really proud of you man, I'm totally going to stop one day too."

2) People say, "I totally quit drinking once too, it was the worst!"

3) People ask, "Are you doing an elimination diet?"

After a few weeks of trying to be normal *and* not drink, I retreated. I went to work, and I went home and snorted coke alone. Some nights I'd drive around just to drive because I couldn't sleep. I'd drive the Colombia River Gorge highway and wait for the sun to rise over the Cascades and Mt. Hood. Even in my loneliness and desperation, these drives soothed me. I was over Portland, but I loved the coast and the mountains.

Things really hit the fan on Halloween. In Portland, Halloween is celebrated with a massive three-day party. I had the night of the 31st off work, so I met up with some of my friends to watch the Phish stream of the Halloween show being held in Vegas. I snorted a ton of coke and was in decent spirits for the first part of the night. We danced in the living room and I was surrounded by people that I loved. Everything seemed okay.

We were supposed to attend a concert which made me anxious from the get-go; I didn't know how to act around a bunch of drunk people and I wasn't sure I'd be able to handle it so I dropped a car load of people off at the Good Foot Lounge and said goodnight. I just sat in my car for a few minutes wondering what I should do next. I went home, put on my roommate's unicorn onesie, snorted some more coke, and hopped back in my car. I drove around aimlessly for a while and eventually wound up where I worked. I walked in the back door to find all of my co-workers sitting at the bar, which was otherwise empty. Everyone knew that I wasn't drinking, so when I walked in, everyone looked at me and went silent. The awkwardness that ensues when normal people are confronted with the sober, big, white unicorn in the room, is painful. I sat at the bar. Of course, they were excited to see me, but I think they could also tell that I was not in a good place. I stayed for a few minutes and smoked some cigarettes. They were all dressed as different characters from Alice in Wonderland, and they looked great. I wanted so badly to drink and be "normal Michael". I wanted to party, talk shit with my friends, dance, fuck some random drunk girl dressed

162

as a slutty bumblebee...I wanted to be *normal*. I went home, alone.

My roommates were gone for the night and as soon as I got home I started chugging wine as hard as I could. I wanted to get sick. I didn't care anymore; I wanted to punish myself and fight the Antabuse. Let me tell you, I lost.

Within minutes, hives appeared all over my face and my heart started pounding through my chest. I started projectile puking all over the backyard. My mind was racing like mad. There was a sick satisfaction in this self-torture, in punishing myself. For what, I still have no idea. I was trapped in a brutal cycle of hating myself for drinking and then drinking because I hated myself. It would take courage to break free from it, and at the time, I had none, with not a lead on where to find it. I kept thinking about how upset I was about how I behaved in Colombia, which would only snowball into thinking about and regretting every single relationship I'd ever been in. I couldn't get past the laundry list of people that I had hurt, offended, accosted, etc. I couldn't conceive what forgiving myself would look like.

Eventually I passed out naked in the bathroom with puke everywhere. When I woke, I had a bloody nose and was brutally hungover. Instead of sobering up and coming to clarity, I was thrown immediately back into a frantic head spin. When I pressed my eyelids closed, visions of past experiences shot across a screen in my mind that wouldn't turn off, and I couldn't avert my eyes. Like the scene from "A Clockwork Orange," my eyes felt clamped open, forced to view all the horrors I'd created, the ones I couldn't change. I saw images from Colombia, past girlfriends, scenes of me acting like a drunken fool. I saw my family, friends, people I missed, wronged, loved, fucked, threw away. It was out of my control. I was losing my mind.

I managed to clean up my mess from the night before, then decided that I was going to kill myself. I thought about hanging myself from the tree in my backyard with one of my surfboard straps, but I didn't want my roommates to find me that way. They'd come home from a good night of partying and go to the backyard to have a cigarette and they'd see me hanging from the fucking tree—I couldn't do that to them. I pictured them trying to cut me down from the tree. I pictured the ambulance showing up and all my meth-head neighbors coming outside to see what was going on. I thought about how they would have to call my mom.

Somehow, I landed on taking a paring knife out of the drawer and going into my room with it. I took my shirt off and wedged it between the closed door of my room and my heart. I started leaning into it and breathing like I would during yoga—I was trying to relax enough and ignore the pinching. I didn't look down. I kept my eyes closed and tried to think happy thoughts. I tried thinking of when I was young, being with both my parents, my sisters. I thought about Jon, and I began to remember how devastating it was when he killed himself. I opened my eyes and looked down at the knife that was a half-inch into my chest with blood dripping down from it. I panicked, stepped back from the door and pulled it out. Then I heard the front door slam and my two roommates walking down the hall. I felt like I was about to be caught jerking off or something, except what I was actually doing was infinitely more humiliating. I threw on a hoodie and walked out into the hallway. I could feel the blood oozing down my chest so I sat down in one of the chairs near the couch and let it collect into my waistband. I talked to them as if nothing had happened.

I don't put much thought into how, why, or when things happen, but thank the universe those two walked in when they did. They asked if I wanted to go to the dive bar a few blocks away for brunch. I went into the bathroom and took off my bloody clothes. I showered and plugged the small hole in my chest with a tampon and medical tape. We drove off to brunch and resumed a normal morning. When we returned, the girls put on a movie in the living room. I went out to the backyard, raked leaves and made a small fire. Then I burnt the bloody clothes in an attempt to erase what had just happened. Somehow, I barely have a scar. I think I've told two people about that morning until writing it now.

Do I really think I was going to kill myself by walking into a paring knife? In retrospect, no. I'm a baby, I hate pain, I hate blood, and that was a fairly dramatic response to something that, in the moment, felt extremely intense. The point is, I'd hit bottom. "Bottom" is different for everyone, but the similarity lies in the way it is utterly lonely down there. No one can hear your pain the way that you feel it. Hitting bottom is like being locked in a soundproof room, trying to scream and realizing your mouth is taped shut, and no one will ever hear you. The room is your mind, and you can't find your way out.

Being suicidal and that level of depression happens—it is a very real thing. In those moments, I wasn't thinking about how much people loved me or the fact that I am a privileged white male from a solid upbringing and could likely get whatever help I needed to figure my shit out. I wasn't thinking about anyone but myself.

The other day, Anthony Bourdain killed himself. This was a major blow to me. Not too long ago, Hanna asked me if I could have anyone's life, who's it would be. I was in the shower and responded without any hesitation, "Anthony Bourdain." Of course, Bourdain's death has been a popular topic of conversation, and one drunk man at the bar the other night where I work kept referring to him as a "pussy." I cringed. I'm cringing now. I was sitting next to this person and I kept my cool. I didn't say a word in response to his assessment of suicide, but what it did was hit a nerve inside me and helped me finish this essay.

Suicide is absolutely selfish, and depression, to some people who are void of certain feelings and awareness, seems like a luxury. I can understand these opinions. My best friend killed himself when I was seventeen. He went into the woods with a shotgun, built a fire, shot himself, and fell into the flames. I was there for the aftermath and I'm still here now. I had a front row seat to the ashes, literal and figurative, that are left behind when someone takes their own life; I'm scarred by it still. However, for people who write off mental illness, to sit around and spout things like, "suicide is the easy way out" or "he was a pussy," that's where I draw the line. If you truly believe that, I envy your ignorance.

Sometimes life is too much for me, so much that I want it to just be over. Be quiet. Be still. When I'm standing at the edge of a cliff staring at the ocean alone, wondering how much the impact would really hurt, or driving down a road and wondering what would happen if I just jerked the wheel a little to the left, I feel ashamed. Mental illness, depression, chronic anxiety and sadness are real. I'll never condone suicide. In my sober, rational mind, I am disgusted by the idea. But I get it. People who have been to the edge know. There are ads for hotlines, support groups, coaches, meetings that might help—use them now. When I was standing in my room alone, deciding that I wanted to die, all the suicide prevention/awareness walks, rubber bracelets, 800-numbers and 5Ks were the last things on my mind.

~

After Halloween, there was a shift in my thinking, I don't remember exactly how or why it happened, but I decided that I didn't want to die, at least not yet. I needed to at least finish grad school. It was going to snow soon and skiing was the one thing I was looking forward to, bum shoulder or not. Luckily, it started snowing right before Thanksgiving. I bought a season pass to Mt. Hood Meadows and started going up two days a week, usually alone. I'd ski in the mornings and I'd work on my thesis at a few different bars in Government Camp in the evenings.

I began seeing a therapist at OHSU that was younger than I was. He did his best, but it was going nowhere. Against his recommendation, I took myself off Antabuse and Lithium and with time, I began to think less about what happened in Colombia and about how depressed I was. The Lithium had made me feel vacant and numb. Maybe it was what I needed for a time, to not feel so much. But I was over it. I started drinking again, pretty much the same way I had before, but I didn't care. I started to feel a bit "normal" again, even if normal wasn't healthy.

I stayed in Portland for Christmas that winter. I didn't want to go home. I knew that if I went to Cleveland for break I'd just black out the entire time, cause scenes, and possibly lose my mind again. Instead, I stuck around Portland and went to a few different holiday parties.

In the way that so many women destroyed me, or rather, I convinced myself that they had, three women saved me. Their names are Chelsey, Michele, and Grey.

Chelsey was my boss and one of four owners at The Observatory, the job that I held almost my entire stint in Portland. She had come from humble beginnings and was a native Oregonian who had seen plenty of shit in her day. She had worked at a number of restaurants in her twenties and eventually got together with her husband and another couple, pooled their money and bought a building in an area or Portland that at that time, wasn't exactly thriving. They built the place from the ground up with their own hands and ran it themselves as owners, servers, bartenders, dishwashers—you name it. Eventually it started to take off and they slowly hired staff, most of which have been there since its inception. These people would later become my family.

Chelsey was militant in the way she ran her restaurant, she demanded perfection from all of us because she cared. She scared the shit out of me at first, so much so that I'd purposely try not to work shifts that she was working because I was so intimidated by her. It was hard to get to know her because she was mostly all business. She had to be, otherwise the place wouldn't be what it is. Over time, Chelsey took to me for whatever reason. Gaining Chelsey's respect was something most people didn't even attempt. She didn't really have favorites, but I felt if she was going to, I would be one of them. She saw me for who I was, she knew everything about me, and she still loved me. She worked me hard, and never let me feel bad for myself. Over time, we became friends. She had a tremendous amount of respect for the fact that I was getting a master's in poetry. She had also learned a lot about my life. She learned about Jon, boarding school, my depression, etc. I guess at the simplest level, she just found me interesting. I adored Chelsey for the fact that she had built one of the most well-known and respected restaurants in Portland from virtually nothing. I quit The Observatory twice while living in Portland, the first was when I had my melt-down in Montana, and the second when I went to Colombia, and she took me back both times. I had to start at the bottom each time I returned, but I did it with gratitude. I am in awe of the fact that she never gave up on me.

While working at The Observatory, one of my co-workers mentioned that I should meet the therapist she was seeing. You can imagine how many times people close to me would tell me this- I blew them off every time. I didn't take recommendations from anyone for anything, but for whatever reason, I took this one. The friend gave me the woman's number. Her name was Grey. I called her one night and we set up an appointment. I'd later find out that Grey was a well-known figure throughout Portland, as she spent several years owning a restaurant and coffee shop before Portland blew up into the food and restaurant mecca it's become now. She saw a variety of clients for many reasons, but her focus was relationships, addiction, depression, and anxiety—a perfect fit.

Ten minutes into my session with Grey I knew she was the one. I feared her right away because I could tell she was going to see right through my bullshit. I dumped everything I had on her that first session. I told her about my parent's divorce, Jon, boarding school, my drinking problem—all the same things I'd told Chelsey about. We had our work cut out for us and I started seeing Grey once a week inside a little shed/office she had beside her house, which was conveniently located two blocks from The Observatory. It seemed to be destiny. Grey helped me understand that I wasn't the fucked-up mess that I believed I was. She began teaching me how to let go of *my story.* She helped me see that I am an extremely compassionate, complex, loving person who is highly sensitive to others and the world around me. She helped me see past a lot of my anger and contempt for the world, and urged me to quit drinking because I could be so much more. Once, she referred to me as "the dog that's constantly barking in the neighbor's yard trying to sound tough and scary, but as soon as you pet it, it rolls over onto it's back because it just wants to be loved."

Grey illuminated the fact that I had been through tremendous loss and trauma, and that it was ok to be a little broken. She helped me work through the process of writing my thesis, and after reading it, she would write one of the most profound responses to my work I'd ever read. Grey kept me alive for those months leading up to my thesis. Every time I'd leave her office I'd be ready to go back to my life with a new confidence. I saw Grey every week until the day I moved to California. We still talk often, and I have been sending her many of these essays. Her favorite, of course, is "Happy Hour with The Universe."

Michele was my poetry professor and thesis advisor at Portland State. I met her for the first time when I first arrived in Portland for a visit. We had coffee on campus and, after reading my writing sample I'd submitted for acceptance into the MFA program said, "There's a lot of trauma, loss, addiction, and anger in your writing, tell me more about this..." I was floored. I thought we were going to shoot the shit about how I like Portland or whatever. This wasn't the case. She asked who I was reading, and of course the answer was "no one." Michele became a sort of

Yoda/mom-away-from-mom the entire time I was in Portland. My poetry was so emotional and personal that often when we'd talk about my work, we were talking about me.

I tried quitting grad school several times. I hated it because I didn't fit in, whatever that means, and because I was constantly challenged on my work, which was a direct reflection of who I was. Every time someone would criticize something I'd written I'd take it personally. This was my fault, but it was hard not to. I constantly fought the system and would regularly have meltdowns, only to have Michele there to calm me down and tell me that I should stop drinking and focus on my work.

Focus on my work, I did. Somehow, I managed to buckle down in school and wrote the hell out of my thesis. I spent most days driving to the coast and surfing after ski season ended and I revised and re-wrote everything I had. It resulted in fifty poems chronicling a lot of what is in this book. I defended on May 21st of 2017.

Defending my thesis was a monumental day. I wore a suit and invited only one friend, Kari. We had a beautiful lunch by the Willamette River, and then Kari listened to me read every single poem aloud at the Rogue Brewery on campus. I sat in the conference room with Michele and the rest of my thesis committee and I talked about my work for over two hours which seemed like five minutes. I signed my defense acceptance that afternoon. After a most unorthodox academic career spanning over nine years, I was finished.

A few weeks before I defended my thesis, April 5, 2017 to be exact, I received an email in response to an essay I submitted to Unsolicited Press offering me a book deal. All I'd ever wanted was the chance to put everything down on paper and release it, the chance to tell the truth, the chance to say I'm sorry and put so much that has been weighing me down for as long as I can remember to rest. It was as though The Universe was finally giving me a break.

On September 16, 2017, a calendar year after that depressing journal entry I'd written, I left Portland. I moved a mile down the road from the entrance to Yosemite National Park, and I started to write this book.

I Am Born

Mom's Version

The summer was long and hot, so hot in fact, I slept with my head at the foot of the bed so I could enjoy an occasional breeze. There were few. I had continued to work until two weeks before you were due. That was the way back in 1986. If it were today, I would have worked all day, cut the grass, fixed the gutters and Uber-ed to the hospital. Being a wee bit of a Type A, I had, of course, packed my "hospital bag" months before. Diapers, bottles, wipes, a blanket and a changing pad would have been it. Nowadays, I would need a trailer to haul all the contraptions that new parents are told they will NEED!

Today, I would have "needed": sterilization devices for everything that touches you, including family members, wipe warmers are a must. The baby should never feel a cold wipe on their precious bottom. As if I do not make enough noise just walking through a room, I would have been told by the experts in safe sleep that I need a White Noise Machine. Anyone who has ever met me knows I do not need noise enhancing products. Many well-meaning friends knit me blankets using WOOL. Such a scandal. Now it must be all cotton gauze like fabric made by folks in India or some other far-reaching country. I have al-

175

ways been a pseudo-researcher; hence the search for a stroller and a car seat was akin to research for one's dissertation. Of course, I had NO idea if you were a girl or a boy, and I am still unclear based on some of your wardrobe choices. So, I settled on a navy-blue stroller that was 95% steel and weighed about forty pounds. It had maroon piping (in case you were a girl). I also secured an umbrella stroller for short jaunts...you never stayed in either.

Now onto bigger issues: The Nursery.

Grandpa Ulinski, always the Polish handyman, was on the caper as we say. He came over and the two of us prepared the room for the Second Coming. We sanded, scraped, and ripped up carpet. After a grueling month of selecting the right décor. I chose a wallpaper with Victorian Children holding hands. I am sure that I still have a sample of it in my hoarding palace. Dad worked endlessly to paint and wallpaper the room. A girl that I worked with had just lost a baby boy, she wanted to have a healing experience and she helped me design your bedding. Her mother (an Italian Grandma) hand sewed your bedding to match the room. The comforter she made has morphed into Gin's "blankie..." the blue one.

Preface: The day before you were born!

Of course, I am always on time…if not early for any event. So…it was 9/26/86.

I had gone to great lengths to be sure all was in place for our baby. I had gone into Mrs. Clean mode. If you knew me then, I was a serious housekeeper. I used to clean the radiators with Q-tips.

Bag packed, house immaculate, laundry done, designated area for baby laundry, car seat in place, stroller in garage and nursery closed off…waiting…waiting. This was necessary because Kelsey insisted on sleeping in your crib. I was so paranoid about the old wives' tales about cats and babies.

We are going to go a few steps backward, which will be necessary for you to understand.

When we married, of course we wanted children. I was surprised when I learned I was going to have a baby. I had felt like I had the flu for six weeks. I thought it was post-holiday blues. I had taken a Friday off from the hospital February 8th to be exact to go on a road trip to the Bureau of Vital Statistics with a friend to pursue adoption records.

Because I had the day off, I rose early and took a pregnancy test (under duress from my wise friends). Low and behold, I was going to be a mom. I got this amazing news the very same day that I found out who my birth mother was. (This is another chapter).

Back to the night before…so there I was watching MASH in the guest bedroom. I had just had a whole and hearty meal of hotdogs and baked beans, watermelon and yes, a root beer float. Just what your OB would advise the night before your baby is due. As the activity on the 4077th was firing up so was the action in my belly. I was not afraid, I had done all the reading so I assumed I was ready!! Ha! Nothing prepares you for childbirth or motherhood.

Around 9:00 p.m. I was getting very uncomfortable, I had showered and called the doctor who advised me (because of insurance) to stay home until after midnight. At this time, I thought it would be wise to let dad know that I was in labor. What do I find? He has been in the basement with a jackhammer all night chopping up a block of cement that our washing machine was on. Oh, by the way it had been there for 30 years. So, in summary, I have a totally trashed, sand filled basement and a very exhausted birth partner. He seemed genuinely aghast that I was in labor on my due date.

On with the night...Dad is less than excited, he is tired, and as you know, when a Murray is tired—the jig is up. Off to Hillcrest we went. Dad drops me off and goes to park the car. Off I went in the wheelchair to labor and delivery. This part I recall like it was yesterday. I was in the bed and things were progressing quickly. Dad was in the room, sleeping. How anyone could sleep through this is way beyond me! In comes a nurse-tech whom I happened to go to high school with. This is when I proceeded to throw up the aforementioned pre-labor dinner. It was not pretty. To her credit, she was awesome!!!

I am progressing as one would expect. The resident said that the baby was BIG (hence your nickname "Fathead") So it is crunch time (not invented then). The resident said we might need to call Dr. Keefe. At this point, I had not felt the need to push, but contractions were coming faster than Superman on speed. They then decided that Radiology would be great fun. It was not. I had to be perfectly still. (I don't do perfectly still on a good day, it was not happening). As it was, I was in transition (baby is imminent), pains are coming and I needed to push. I might add that I saw you on this x-ray; you became a real little person. I saw you moving inside me and sucking your thumb while in utero. It was the coolest thing and I was watching this while trying to focus on delivering you!!!

At this time, I was ready. They called Dr. Keefe to come in. To me, the new mom, this is a BIG RED FLAG. In comes Dr. Keefe in full scrubs and ready to roll. The bad news is that my pelvic measurements were too small to accommodate this baby, the good news was, based on an exam, I was having a boy! I was so thrilled—I knew in my heart you were boy. I wanted a boy first, I was elated. The so-called bad news was I would need a C-section. With my pseudo-medical background, I was happy to have the option because I wanted a healthy baby. I did not need to be a hero. I wanted safe. I would deal with post-op recovery, but save the baby from undue trauma.

The first order of business was getting an epidural. This is a tricky endeavor under the best of circumstances. Dr. Keefe asked us if we would be willing to let a resident place the catheter. Before I had a second to think about it, dad firmly said no. The next hour or so was a blur. Lots of clinking and banging, and there you were. A lusty cry, the second Apgar Score was perfect. They showed you to me and off you went to be weighed (8lb 14oz) with a head circumference of six-hundred inches. You had a fat head! You were twenty-one inches. You're left testicle was completely bruised and swollen and your right hip was dislocated, hence your leg-length discrepancy and hip issues. You were what is called a frank breech, which meant you were sort of folded in half and coming butt first. This probably set the tone for much of your life. They took you to the newborn nursery. Dad went with you and back to the room. The next hour was spent putting the stuffing back in Mrs. Scarecrow. (ME). It was now around 11:00 am.

I slept for a while, but couldn't wait to hold you. I never wanted to put you down. I had absolutely no idea what to do with you but it all came very naturally. Despite you being a "big" baby, you were so tiny. You looked so fragile and unspoiled, just beautiful. C-Section babies are prettier than normal delivery babies; you aren't beat up, you had big rosy cheeks and a cap of fine fuzz on your head. I wanted to keep you close and never let go (I still feel that way some-times). The nurses had to convince me to put you in the nursery so I could sleep. I listened, but wasn't happy. Recovery was not fun, but they get you up and moving the next day. I think that Grandpa Murray and Granny were your first visitors. Grandpa Murray was a natural with babies.

My mom came but seemed afraid to hold you. This was probably reflective of the depression that was soon to overcome her. My friend Molly had just had a baby boy a few doors down and she came to greet you. Sadly, this friend has recently been diagnosed with Alzheimer's disease. Jack and Peggy came to see you. I was told that Jack NEVER goes to hospitals, but he toughed it out to see Big Red's baby. I was in the hospital for five days and couldn't wait to get you home. I wanted to see you in your little room. I recall that it was summer leaving the hospital when we went to have you and in those five days it had become Indian Summer. It was a lovely time of year to walk a new baby proudly through the tree-lined streets of our neighborhood. Of course, you had your days and nights mixed up, as many babies do. I was sleep deprived, but I cherished the nights that I rocked you in your room. I would look out at the street lamp on Glendon and think I was the luckiest mom in the world. I had YOU.

Dad's Version

When your Mom and I got married we both agreed on a plan: We would live in her apartment for one year to save money for a down payment on a house. We bought the house on Glendon one year later. We planned on living in the house for a year before having children. You were born one year later. The pregnancy was pretty normal as I remember. We attended Lamaze classes, which would later prove to be in vain.

I don't remember the week leading up to your birth as I went to work every day and came home at night to help out. All in all, a pretty normal week. I remember getting jumpy, so I chose a project to work on that Friday night. The old washing machine was mounted on a concrete pad that was around eight inches thick. I went down into the basement with a sledge hammer to pound the pad down to nothing. It took several hours of swinging the hammer to accomplish this task. I finished around 10:00 p.m. covered in sweat, concrete dust, and totally exhausted. All I wanted to do was take a shower and collapse into bed. Then your mom told me it was time to go to Hillcrest Hospital. I said, "you're kidding right?" She wasn't.

I could barely stay awake to drive to the hospital. We went up to the OB/maternity floor and I think they paged the doctor. I was having a hard time staying awake and probably kept dozing off while we waited for the doctor to get to the hospital. The doctor arrived around 1:00 or 2:00 am. He determined that your mom needed an X ray to determine if you could fit through the birth canal. We went down to Radiology for that. Then we had to wait several more hours for a Radiologist to read the film. The result: your head would not fit through the birth canal, hence the nickname, "Fathead."

Your mom was put on the surgery schedule for an emergency C-section. Again, I kept dozing in and out of consciousness. The surgery went as planned and you were born that morning. That's when they noticed the thing with your hip displacement. I remember the whole event being surreal. It was like living in a dream between the events happening and being exhausted. The memories are kind of hazy. I think that when your mom got to her hospital room, I passed out in a chair. Your mom was so relieved to have the birth over and excited to have you born. I was relieved, excited, and exhausted. It took a little while for everything to sink in. It felt strange taking you home and putting you into your crib. There was this new person in our house after living there with just the two of us. The joy started to sink in. There was this new baby to love and take care of. We were both overjoyed. Life felt pretty good and complete. It still does even after all these years. Love you. I'm proud of you.

My Jon

Jon was my best friend and the closest thing I'll ever have to a brother.

He killed himself March 6th, 2004.

If you ask me for physical proof that we were best friends, brothers, or otherwise, I have none. There are a few pictures floating around somewhere. After he died, this was all taken from me.

I used to have his suicide note along with some burnt pieces of his clothing, but I threw them out some years back.

What I do have are my memories with him. These are mine—they are all I have left of him—and I'm keeping them for myself.

My Entire Life Before My Eyes

"I had always heard your entire life flashes before your eyes the second before you die. First of all, that one second, isn't a second at all, it stretches on forever, like an ocean of time."

-Lester Burnham from *American Beauty*

Here's how I imagine my ocean of time might look:

Feeding ducks with mom at Wade Oval my blue bike with training wheels Glendon Road the elevator ride to the maternity ward to meet newborn Megan bowling at The Colony sisters greeting the horses at the fence with fistfuls of apples and carrots the saltwater fish tank in grandma and grandpa's condo lobby and

four-year-old Kaki fearlessly chucking herself off the high dive at Pervis

grandma's waffles and my very own powdered sugar shaker

Lake Lucerne and sitting on dad's lap with a sucker in my mouth getting our hair cut by Joe Dauria and breathing in the smells at Dunn Hardware

fresh cut wood

power tools
and little Gin being wheeled around the house in
mom's custodian bucket with her snowman cast on
Blockbuster trips with dad watching *Blue Velvet,*
Apocalypse Now, Kingpin, Stripes, Austin Powers
mom playing air guitar with her mop to Eric Clap-
ton's VH1 Unplugged
Camp Onyahasa
Skiing with dad for the first time
   Falling
      Falling
        Falling
          —he never let me quit.

The lacrosse state championship trophy and picking
John Carroll's nose in the quad and
Pizza Hut breadsticks from the In-Between
rollerblades everywhere
throwing snowballs at campus security kissing girls
in front of the Blessed Virgin statue popcorn chicken
at Thorton listening to DMX skating holding girls'
hands and foxtrotting with debutants at Junior Dance
and Holtz singing louder than anyone at Gesu music
shows and mass

Geraci's restaurant

Arabica, bikes everywhere payphone calls to girls
from the vestibule War Heads candy from Olga the
sweaty Russian lady at Shaker Deli stolen Black and
Mild's from Campus Drug cigarettes from the old
machine in the Pizzazz basement and Phish for the
first time with Benacci

Jon Marshall

Listening to Phish with Craig on the way to school
the sold-out Grog Shop shows with Quadrophonic, X's
on our hands Meggie's garage AKA Steak's Apartment and that moose crossing Lake Flagstaff

Seabrook with Amy and Danielle and pistachios on
the patio with Fritz listening to Jazz with our single
malt scotch on Fripp

Adelay

John Carroll diploma
dean's list   a hug from the dean
the entire ceremony's pause
Megan's scene from Chicago in acting class
my first wave
holding Bucky's newborn
Jeff, Josh and Hanna, eggnog, and cheer on that
Christmas Eve

B and Lady playing in mom's backyard

Wine and dancing to Rod Stewart on
    our first night in the new house
        just a mattress on the floor
        a fire to keep us warm

And mom-
    oh my mom.
            My best friend
            my biggest fan
            my partner in crime.

            My breath
            My mom.

"I guess I could be pretty pissed off about what happened to me, but it's hard to stay mad when there's so
much beauty in the world. Sometimes I feel like I'm
seeing it all at once, and it's too much; my heart fills
up like a balloon that's about to burst. And then I
remember to relax, and stop trying to hold onto it.
And then it flows through me like rain, and I can't
feel anything but gratitude—for every single moment of my stupid, little life."

                                    -Lester Burnham

My Anxiety, My Self

As far back as I can remember, I've been an anxious person. In the early years, I self-soothed by chewing my fingernails. When my mom wasn't scratching my back so I could fall asleep, or allowing me to sit in her lap and obsessively twirl her hair, I gnawed at my nails. Eventually, I gnawed one aggressively enough to require minor surgery to correct an infection. Because of this, I have a mangled finger; it looks like I spilled corrosive acid over it. I literally refer to it as "my grotesque."

In my early youth, I was also angry. My mom tells me that when I was born I was "mad as thunder." Soon after, anger would mix with worry and anxiety and I would take it out on myself. When I was about five, and didn't know what to do with these feelings, I would bang my head against the brick garage in our backyard. I'd hit myself at school and slam my head against anything near me in an attempt to calm the circus that was, and is, my mind.

My parents, understandably, were more than a little concerned. They brought me to child psychiatrists at the Cleveland Clinic for observation. I'd sit and play with toys and talk with therapists while both doctors and my parents would watch through a one-way window. We had special meetings with teachers who, at the time, were conservative nuns, I had to see school appointed shrinks, the whole nine yards...But my anger and self-abuse didn't add up; I played normally with other kids, I never harmed anyone but myself, I wasn't raised in an abusive family, but right out of the gates, I was angry, and anxious. The doctors' prescription was to put me on stimulants.

All of this special attention started to take a toll on my psyche. I was being conditioned to feel and think that there was something wrong with me. I had to take special pills that no one else was taking, attend special meetings, see special specialists...it didn't feel special at all. I was smart enough to recognize that I was being labeled as "the bad kid." It was at this early age that I started writing the script for a story I would hang on to with death-grips for the rest of my life:

No one will love me.
People will judge me.
I'm different.
I don't deserve love.

My early physical mutilation and head-banging would soon transform into cutting. I carved lines into my skin with rocks to make them look like the normal wear-and-tear a young boy would accumulate. I remember the feeling of relief as I'd drag sharp stones across my skin—it would hurt for a second, then I'd feel strangely satisfied, pacified. Later on, the physical would turn into mental mutilation.

Once I was older, it became clear to me that it was socially unacceptable to bang my head against walls and cut myself—that's when I found drugs. Drugs seemed to help me interact with other people, because they temporarily lessened the intensity of my anxiety.

When difficult things happened, even events that were completely out of my control, my story that "*I* am a fuck up...there's something wrong with *me*" would flare. When my parents split up, and it seemed that everyone's attention was on our family's narrative, I felt the familiarity of being labeled as different. I dug deeper into drowning my sorrows with weed and booze. All this did was get me into trouble with school and the law; it was a self-fulfilling prophecy that was *my story.* In my mind, everyone already thought I was a joke, so it became the easiest role for me to fulfill, and still, I couldn't understand why I was constantly filled with anxiety. I carried these feelings with me for my adolescence and into my twenties, and eventually I found Yoga.

Now, I don't want this essay to become one of the hundreds of "my journey to Yoga" stories, but hear me out. A handful of tragic (and out of my control) events occurred in one compact month that sent me into a fit of deep sadness and depression. In an attempt to help me, a friend's mother bought me a Yoga Fusion class package. I originally agreed to attend the classes with hopes of picking up women, but something unexpected happened—I started *feeling* a little better. The ninety minutes of breathing and physically exerting myself was calming my mind, if only for a short period of time. Yoga became the only thing that would squelch my anxiety a little, aside from what I thought booze and drugs were doing for me. It was the first time I invested any thought into really wanting to fix myself. It's funny because the obvious things like quitting smoking or drinking weren't on my radar at all. All I wanted to do was fix my head. I didn't know at that point that drinking was fueling my anxiety, I just knew Yoga was helping a little bit.

As with most things that I "like," I overdid Yoga. I became addicted to the positive feeling I'd reach during and briefly after and started attending the hardest classes I could find. Sometimes, I'd go to three classes in a day. Eventually, I'd become a certified Yoga instructor, and immediately following graduation I'd suffer from a Yoga related injury to my left shoulder which resulted in surgery. In hindsight, I was returning to my tendency to self-mutilate, but this time it seemed "healthy."

I spent the summer in a sling drinking strawberry, banana, Oxycodone smoothies while watching Game of Thrones. Even after my recovery period was over, and I could have continued to pursue Yoga, I returned to drinking hard. Eventually, I'd focus all my efforts into a new crusade of trying to prove to everyone in my Cleveland community that I wasn't a fuckup by applying to grad schools and I'd lose sight of Yoga.

When I got into grad school and moved to Portland, I tried Yoga again. I attempted to pick up right where I left off, with the *healthy* wailing on myself, and almost immediately injured my other shoulder. Cue the violins. Pour the Bourbon. Enter, anxiety.

A few months ago, I decided to stop drinking. No Antabuse, no AA meetings. It dawned on me that drinking alcohol was literally pouring anxiety, fear, anger and sadness down my throat. A few weeks later, I began noticing my anxiety starting to abate. I was sleeping better, I felt less worry and stress, and I began feeling less shameful. I was rewriting *my story* and I didn't even know it.

I've attempted drinking again several times, and the results have always been the same: I hate myself afterwards, I get anxious and depressed, I say stupid shit, and I forget most of what I do. Testing the alcoholic waters again was like an itch that I needed to satisfy. I had to see and feel *for sure* that it doesn't work for me. Turns out, even drinking a little is a form of self-torture and mental mutilation. I know now that that was part of my old story I'm ready to rewrite.

I can't say that my anxiety is gone. Writing this essay is giving me anxiety. This book is giving me anxiety. I'm hyper aware of what people might say. I get the obsessive, frantic, thought reel from time to time. *People are going to read this...People might hate this book...People might hate me...* All of those things are out of my control. I've been trying to focus on what *is* in my control; I've been trying to focus. It sometimes works.

Before I sat down to write this essay I had to first drive to get a coffee, have a cigarette, start laundry and clean the kitchen. Maybe it's just avoidance, but now I'm sitting here thinking about the wet clothes in the dryer and it's giving my anxiety. It's one of those itches I need to satisfy. One of those tricks my brain plays—but it isn't torture. I'm not locked in a padded room of my own making. I can speak, and hear, and think, and love and stay grateful. I can feel anxious *and* feel happy too. I can contain madness and talent, compassion, empathy, and love. Sometimes, even a little for myself. I still struggle with finding a balance between accepting myself and drowning in the curse of being myself. But I can live with that.

So, I've decided to stay.

The thing is, the alternative would have been to make all of this meaningless; all the places and heart spaces where I've appeared as an emotional buffoon, a drunk, a connector, a friend, an everything—to prove that it really is all just too much. And as satisfied as I'd have been to fulfill the poetic tragedy in all of that, The Universe had other plans for me. I suppose I did too.

I think I'll always be an anxious person, but I'm learning how to be with human feelings, without getting hammered all the time. I've come a long way, and I have a long way to go, but luckily, I've still got time to rewrite my story. My biggest fear *is* being happy. What this might look like is forgiving myself for all the shameful and disgusting, spiteful, anger-driven things I've done over the last few decades. I suppose this book will attempt to say 'I'm sorry' to everyone. I suppose this book might help me say 'I'm sorry' to myself. I suppose, in some way, this book is my own version of rehab. All I can do is keep trying.

-The Beginning-

Acknowledgements

Love and thanks to:

Unsolicited Press

The English departments at John Carroll University and Portland State University

Ken Alexander

Grey Wolfe

Chelsey Warriner and everyone at The Observatory

Michele Glazer

Sergeant Ed Matousek

Dr. Christopher Roark

Geraci's Restaurant

Gesu Catholic School and every friend I made there

The Hyde Wilderness School Staff, especially the Devlin family, Johanna Sorrell, and Amy Griffin Atchley

Tom Hayes, Brian Macaskill and Phil Metres

Pat and Sandy Hanrahan

Halle

Joan Doyle AKA Grambe, you are in my heart

The Spoths, Laverys, Salatas, Hills, Bacons, Holzheimers and Villaires

The brothers Votruba and Lizzie

Jenna

Margot McKeegan and the Gruttadauria family

Katie, Grayson and Adelay

The Ertel family
Linda and Cody Serio
Kari and Aaron Voegele
My Portland family, you know who you are
Kate, Brooke, Tim, Matt and Paloma
Lebs AKA Ryan Garson
Marie Ann Leo
The Mueller family
Chrissie Lanzieri
Meg Kokovai, for being honest and unmerciful
Tom Hamilton of *Brothers Past*, whose music I listened to
while writing, thinking about and editing this book
Josh Foley, for instilling a love of food, wine, and hospitality and providing a space for me to write
Jeff Fauk, for keeping me laughing all the time and for
always reminding me never to take myself too seriously
My grandfather Edward Ulinski

My family, especially Kaki, whose pure, unconditional love
and adoration encourages me to stay, just as I am

And Hanna, for finding me again when I was lost, jumping
into this ocean with me and giving The Universe my number

About the Author

Michael Murray is a writer from Cleveland and currently lives in California near Yosemite National Park.

Instagram: @writingnaked
Email: writingnakedmichaelmurray@gmail.com

About the Press

Unsolicited Press started without the bootstraps in California in 2012, and has progressed to publish out-of-this-world fiction, creative nonfiction, and poetry. The team refuses to accept industry standards and acquires quirky, phenomenal, and true art from authors around the world. Learn more at www.unsolicitedpress.com.

Made in the USA
San Bernardino, CA
31 December 2018